PUBLISHED by PARABLES
Earthly Stories with a Heavenly Meaning

Frederick Demerchant

THE ROAD TO REDEMPTION
BY
FREDERICK DEMERCHANT

PUBLISHED by PARABLES
Earthly Stories with a Heavenly Meaning

Frederick Demerchant

The Road To Redemption
Frederick Demerchant

Published By Parables
August, 2022

Printed in the United States of America

Readers should be aware that Internet Web sites offered as citations and/or sources for further information may have been changed or disappeared between the time this was written and the time it is read.

THE ROAD TO REDEMPTION
BY

FREDERICK DEMERCHANT

PUBLISHED by PARABLES
Earthly Stories with a Heavenly Meaning

Frederick Demerchant

The Road To Redemption

(By Frederick DeMerchant)
Chapter 1: rain and tears are coming down.

On an extremely rainy cold night, a mid Novembers night in Halifax Nova Scotia Troy Lewis was just bout at the end of his rope. He had a glock in his Rain drenched overcoat pocket. And a voice just kept saying, pull the trigger Loser, pull the trigger loser!!!!!Take it out of your pocket put it in your mouth And pull that trigger!!! Troy did consider doing that as he walked along Abrams way.But as he put his hand into his pocket to grab the glock. All Of a sudden something flooded and i mean flooded his mind. On a hill far away stood an Old rugged cross the emblem of suffering and shame.And I love that old cross Where the dearest and best for a world of lost sinners was slain. So ill cherish The old rugged cross. Till my trophies at last i'll lay down. I will cling to the old rugged cross and exchange it one day for a crown. As these words were in his mind, many things took place. He began to cry profusely He thought of being Ten years old sitting in church with his grammy on a sunday night. He thought i just had 3 guys beat the tar out of me. With a black eye broken nose and sore ribs to show for it. I carry this glock for protection, but why

1

didn't i draw it And blow those guys away? I didn't cry during my beating ,why am I crying now?And he thinks at 38 this hurt a lot worse then it seemed to when it happened when i was 25.He sees a park bench and he sits down. He holds His head in his hands and he cries and cries and cries!!!

His mind goes to many many thoughts. He thinks of Madeline and her beautiful smile.From grade 11 until they said i do, in their 20th year of life.

The days that they went to church every sunday morning,to his logging job layoff.To the tragic night madeleine was taken from him feb 8th ,2002.

He had called her up from his part time job at the shell gas station. Life didn't seem bad.She was finishing up her last year of lpn nursing.She baby sat

Thursday and Friday evenings. They were getting by. They were talking and had made an agreement to go out for valentines day on feb 14th 2002 to a nice restaurant called Paul's diner.2 hrs later madeline was dead from a car accident She hit a patch of black ice and crashed down over an embankment.

She was dead on impact.Finally his tears began to stop flowing.His ribs hurt alot.His nose hurt worse.But his heart seemed to hurt the worst. How did i even get here he thought to himself.Perhaps he made all these poor choices because of a broken heart over the loss of madeline.Perhaps it was the lure of easy money.Perhaps it was an easy road to a better life..

Transporting drugs from Halifax n.s. To boston mass twice a week.Troy's dad   Came from st.stephen new brunswick.His mom came from woodland maine.

So crossing the border twice a week was no big deal.He had family from woodland maine to augusta maine,he could say he was visiting.And the 6 yr old toyota corolla maine plated that he had at his cousins i n lincoln maine,certainly wasn't suspicious on the big interstate 95 that led to boston.And besides Troy was born in calais maine.His parents deliberately did This for 3 reasons.His mom was a head executive at the big georgia pacific mill in woodland maine.She had great benefits which included medical.So if your born in america your automatically an american citizen.The 2nd reason

The Canadian government looked on Troy as a Canadian citizen born abroad. Where as his dad was a canadian citizen born in st .stephen new brunswick Canada.So in his life he could enjoy citizenship from 2 countries,america and Canada.And the 3rd reason was it would give him the right to work or live or study in either Canada or the united states.A world of opportunities more than most people get to enjoy in this life. So how on earth did he end up soaking wet on the verge of catching pneumonia ,busted,broke and beaten up on a park bench in Halifax Nova Scotia?

It certainly was no easier road.It certainly was no road to riches.He might have had enough change in his pocket to purchase a medium coffee from tim hortons.If he could be lucky enough to find one that is open this time of night.Troy rubs his eyes and stands to his feet.He remembers something his grammy taught him years ago.How to pray to God. God if your listing this is Troy,Troy Lewis. God i've made such a mess of my life.But tonight my life could

Have and should have been taken from me but it wasn't. God if you can some how forgive me and help me to clean up the mess i've made of my life. Help Me to get out of this mess ive made of my life.Help me to get out of this

Awful situation, I promise you ill live for you,and serve you for the rest of my life.Troy puts each hand in his jeans pockets.He pulls out what change is in each pocket.He sits back down and begins to count.A dollar eighty eight and one more dime makes a dollar ninety eight. This will definitely get me a medium coffee.Now if i can just find a tim hortons that is open.As he walks along the cold lonely street of abrams way as he tops the hill he cant believe his eyes..Off in the distance he sees a tim hortons sign and under it it says open 24 hours.A refreshing glimmer of hope of what was an extremely rough night!!! He makes his way to the door.There is one car idling in the parking lot. And two flatbed tractor trailers loaded with mactara lumber out of upper musquodoboit Nova Scotia.There is a little baby being bounced in her mothers arms The baby is gently crying and her mom is trying to soothe her.

Behind her is a middle aged man he's wearing a dickies sweater half tucked in and half not tucked in.He is wearing ripped jeans and a pair of greb work boots. Perhaps he's getting done with the afternoon shift from 4pm to midnight at the Ikea furniture store factory whereas his shoulders have a lot of sawdust on them.

And behind him was a big man he stood about 6ft 3 inches tall and weighed About 245 lbs.Salt and pepper hair with a salt and pepper beard to match.

He turned around and looked at Troy.He smiled and said hello.Troy just nodded his head.The lady ordered and left,then the guy with the greb work boots. Then it was the big mans turn.Good evening a friendly cashier says

Good evening heather, how are you? The big man smiles and says.Im good thank you Paul. Where are you off to tonight?Junior and I are off to the same spot we have to be in Anderson, South Carolina for 9am Monday morning.

Well i wish you both safe travels heather smiles and replies.I wish these guys would quit chit chatting and hurry up!!! Troy thinks to himself.Thanks heather

I appreciate that! I'll have 2 large double doubles and an old fashioned sugar donut please.Is that it heather smiles and asks?No no it's not whatever this gentleman would like to.Ok heather replies. Hi sir. Excuse me sir. Paul steps to the side.Sir excuse me.YAA?!!!! Troy belts out.Your order sir what would u like?I would like a medium coffee black with one sugar .Sure, anything else asks heather?what? Replies Troy. Heather smiles and says is there anything else you would like sir?

No that's it replies Troy.Paul interrupts .You can eat a sandwich can't you?

I umm I.Sure he can .What kind would you like ?Asks Paul to Troy.I don't have

Money for a sandwich.Says Troy.Thats ok replies heather .Pauls picking up Your tab tonight.Troy was so caught up in his current situation and current Thoughts that he didn't even hear what Paul said.How he was gonna pay for his order.I'll have a ham and cheese please.Troy looked at Paul,broken swollen nose and all and said thank you.

Thank you sir.Paul smiles and says you are most welcome.As his sandwich Is being made,Troy sits down in his soaking clothes,puts his head down near his chest and begins to cry again.But not because of sadness this time . But Simply because of love!! It had been a long time a lot of years actually since anyone had shown Troy any type of kindness.Let alone a coffee and a sandwich .As the sandwich is being made heather hands it over to Paul.Paul Pays his tab and hands the sandwich over to Troy.Thank you,Troy looks and says with wet tear filled eyes.Paul smiles and says your welcome.Troy goes out to the parking lot,peels the wrapper back off his sandwich and stands there and eats it.At least the rain has stopped he thought to himself..Back inside the donut shop heather looks at Paul and says ,well it looks like the rain is stopping and the fog is starting to lift.Yes this is great replies Paul..

Makes it a lot easier for trucking.Ibet heather smiles and says!! Outside Troy finished scarfing down his sandwich
He can't remember when the last time was that he had one that tasted so good!!

But when your life consists of booze,cocaine and running with the devil.A nice good sandwich probably wasn't a priority!!

As Troy is drinking away his coffee,Paul comes out and says i'm glad the rain and fog has lifted.It makes it a lot easier for me to drive.Hay mister thanks for the coffee and sandwich. I really appreciate it!Hay it's my pleasure Paul smiles and says..How tall are you? He asks Troy.

I'd say 5ft 7 5ft 8 ? I'm 5ft 9 . I was close says Paul.Why don't you come over to my truck,im sure junior has

Some clothes that are nice and dry that will fit you. Get you out of these cold wet ones you have on. As they walk over to Pauls truck as there walking up to it,Paul stops and gently Knocks on the sleeper compartment door of the truck parked in front of Pauls.

A young man around 24 or 25 gets out of the sleeper compartment and sits in the driver's seat and rolls down his window.here you go son.Paul smiles and says a nice double double for you.And one old fashioned sugar donut.Aww thanks dad i really really appreciate it the man smiles and says.Who is your new friend?You know i dont believe ive caught his name. Paul smiles and says.

While this is going on Troy reads the lettering on the door of the truck; Paul macallister and son transport ltd.Paul extends his hand to Troy young man im Paul ,Paul mcallister nice to meet you. Troy shakes his hand and replies nice to meet you. I'm Troy Lewis.The young man extends his hand out the side window and shakes Troy's hand. Nice to meet you im Paul macallister jr. Troy shakes his hand im Troy Lewis he replies. Paul asks Junior if he has any extra clothes in there. This young man is about your size and he's drenched.

I have a pair of jogging pants, a t- shirt and a sweater.
He could have. Replied Paul junior Can you get them
for us? Sure dad.As Troy and Paul wait while junior
goes back in the bunk to get the clothes.Troy asks Paul,
where are you guys off to tonight?

We are both delivering in the same spot, replies Paul.
We unload in anderson south carolina at 9 am on
monday morning.Here you go dad, says junior as he
hands Paul down the clothes.Thanks very much son

.As Paul hands them to Troy he says why don't you go
into the washroom in tims and put these nice dry clothes
on?Ok good idea replies Troy.He makes his way into
the washroom Paul says to him. Hey Troy?Yes, replies
Troy. You need a ride somewhere?Troy thinks to
himself for a second.I definitely don't wanna Stay
around here.He looks back at Paul and says yes sir i'll
catch a ride with you after i change.Shure just jump in
my truck when you come out Paul smiles and says i'll
do up my log book while i am waiting for you... As Troy
goes into the washroom and peels out of his wet
clothes.He grabs paper towel from the paper towel
dispenser and tries to dry off the best that he can.As he
is folding up his coat his glock falls out of his
pocket,onto

The floor and its loaded. Whoa, I'm glad the safety was
on!!!!Otherwise it may have went off then id have
another huge mess to contend with!As he removes The
clip he thinks about the prayer he prayed to god!!He

removes the clip goes into the garbage bin and moves the top 7 or 8 pieces of paper towel. He takes all 6 bullets out of the clip.Throws them into the garbage barrel. And then throws the pieces of paper towel back on top of them again.

So that nobody will see the bullets.He puts the empty clip back into the gun.and places it back into his coat pocket He folds up his coat then places it along with the rest of his clothes into the bag that Paul jr had given him.As he walks back out and gets into Pauls truck

Paul has the heat cranked right up.You got it nice and warm in here wouldn't you say?asks Troy to Paul..Paul smiles and says if it gets to hot in here for you,turn the blower motor down a notch or crack a window.Thats what i love about these freightliner classic trucks ,the heaters in them work great!!!

Excuse me, says Paul as he grabs the cb mike .How bout it, junior, do you have a copy?Go ahead dad .Troy and i are all set are you ready to roll. 10-4 dad the voice over the air replies.Troy says to Paul. Don't worry about the heat Paul I Love the warmth.Paul replies me to! As they get out onto the trans Canada highway,and head west,Paul asks Troy a few questions..Young man if you don't mind me saying,i can see your eye is in bad shape and id say that your nose is broken.Troy looks out the passenger side window through the night.Id say your about right mister. Replied Troy. Well would you like me to drop you off

At the hospital in moncton? No thank you replies Troy. This is the 3rd time my nose has been broken. It will heal.I'll be ok. Will you be ok? Asks Paul/ As that old truck roars through the night,tears fall out of the eyes of Troy,he sure hopes he will.Troy rubs his eyes.Oh ya oh ya it will.I Have been praying to god you know Troy tells Paul.Praying asks Paul? When did you start that?Well i used to do it alot with my grammy when i was little says Troy.Many a year has passed since that but i've recently started again says Troy.Paul has both his big ole hands on the steering wheel guiding that load of lumber down the road but he removes the right one and gently puts it on Troy's shoulder.That's great son thats really great keep praying.I will Troy smiles and says. Where are you crossing into the United States at? We cross the border at calais maine Paul replies.Paul looks at Troy and says i just got a brand new therapeutic mattress

That's really comfortable, why don't you kick off your shoes and lay down for a while? Troy was so happy that Paul would offer that to him.Troy looks over at Paul and says maybe i will. Troy was so so so happy that Paul had offered that to him.As Troys taking off his shoes he looks over at Paul and asks him about 10 mins before you come into saint john new brunswick could you wake me up? No problem Paul replies.I like to drive to a little music would it bother you if i put it on low? No not at all replied Troy.As Troy gets into the bunk and pulls the curtain shut,as his sore aching body sank into that mattress, he thought about how it felt to be in a warm safe comfortable place, and it felt fantastic.As he layed there he thought i'm rolling down a highway, but i'm safe and im warm!!!! In no time

Flat he falls asleep.It seems like its no time at all and he hears a voice call his name.Troy, hey Troy.Yes Troy shouts out im about 10 or 12 minutes outside

Saint john says Paul.Ok thank you says Troy. As Troy lays there he thinks to himself if I'm around saint john I'm still close to those guys.   Where could i Go to make a new start? He pulls open the bunk curtain. Hey Paul, could I ask you something? Sure pal replies Paul.Are you stopping anywhere before you cross the border into the usa? Well we usually sleep a cppl hours at the red rooster truck stop then get up fuel up and cross the border.Ok well when i was

Little i grew up in st stephen.My Passport is at my moms house. Would you mind if i walked down to my moms house and got it and caught a ride into the usa with you?No, that's fine, says Paul but 2 questions for you. How far is your moms house from the red rooster? Not far says Troy i can walk it in 20 or 25 mins,each way.and second question. I don't mind giving you a ride, but you might have some trouble at the border,Whys that asks Troy?Well you have a black eyes and a broken swollen nose replies Paul.The customs officers may See you as undesirable.Ican wait a few mins but if they are going to hold you

Up quite a long time, we have to go , we are on a scheduled run.They cannot deny me entry into the usa replied Troy im a citizen i was born in calais maine.

Ok no problem says Paul you can go with me as far as you want.Thank you Very much Troy smiles and says.No problem says Paul. Go back to sleep if you want and i'll wake you up at the red rooster.Thank you, says Troy. As Troy Lays back down he thinks to himself winter will be upon us soon.Maybe way

Down south would be a great place to make a new start.No bad actors knew him or knew of him down in that country.He promised God if he would help him
He would serve him and love him the rest of his days.The reason that Troy had to endure that bad beating was because he was given $35000 ,worth of street valued cocaine. The drop was boston same as always.After being 2 days late

And snorting about $900 worth up his nose,the boys in Boston are saying $17500 the shipment is missing.Half the shipment but that wasn't true$900 dollars worth did go up Troy's nose.But that's a far cry from $17500.

The Halifax to Boston cocaine smuggling trade was about a 9.5 million dollar a year business. So you can bet the powers to be in Halifax Nova Scotia didn't like to hear that half a shipment did not arrive.Now the shipment did arrive in full ,all but the $900 worth that Troy snorted up his nose.But the pickup man that they had sent this time Troy had never dealt with him before.Also Troy always

Always drops in revere Massachusetts his very first drop and everyone he has ever done has always been Revere. But this new guy was adimate about meeting in Peabody. Now the cocaine trade definitely has some shady characters .But something was definitely aloof this time.The boys in Halifax

Want $17500 as soon as possible or the broken nose,blackeye,and sore ribs is just a taste of what is to come.But Troy has no idea of what is going on.He drifts off back to sleep.Troy, hay Troy buddy we are at the red rooster. Oh oh um ok thanks Paul replied Troy.Troy gets up grabs the plastic bag tells Paul he will be back in around an hour and he strikes out for his mom and dad's house.

About half way there Troy steps off into the woods,he takes his jeans out of the bag and uses them for a rag.He wipes the prints off the glock as best he can Then with his bare hands hes digs down about 10 to 11 inches into the earth.It is almost ready to crack daylight.He looks all around there there isn't a soul around but him ,and whatever critter may be lurking in the woods watching him.Ok God i didn't just pray it says Troy im trying to live it.He drops the glock into the shallow grave and covers it over as quick as he can.

Chapter 2: the southland welcomes a northerner.

When Troy endured that bad bad beating in Halifax Nova Scotia.most people would have pulled that glock out of there pocket and started pumping out bullets.Now not this time, but Troy did draw that gun before,and he pumped out bullets.Lots and lots of bullets.But the last time he was in a rest area washroom in haverhill Massachusetts at 127am and two guys tried to rob him of $35000 in cash. Things got bad. Things got very very very bad very very quickly!!!These people must have tailed him from the drop point,or was it enforcers for the same people he sold the doap to in the first place? One will never know!! But Troy did know that they jumped him in the restroom And he also knows that the rest areas in massachusetts have no cameras

Like the ones in New hampshire do. But after that, all rest areas in the state of Massachusetts now have cameras. Troy shot both men who jumped him that nite with the glock he just buried.He had heard later on that one guy got out with a lot of damage to his right chest and right shoulder but the other man never got out he was dead before his body ever hit the floor Troy fired 5 bullets from that glock that night. 1 into the chest and one into the shoulder of the guy that lived .one into the neck "particularly the juggler area" and 2 into the left collarbone area the guy never had a chance or a hope. He was dead before he hit the floor.As soon as Troy broke free from both men and shot them that nite, he ran fast and hard to his car and he didn't stop driving his car until he got all the way to newport maine where he stopped to get gas at the newport irving.He nervously pumped his gas at the newport irving watching everybody watching there every move. Troy gassed up grabbed a coca cola out of the cooler paid his bill and never stopped till be pulled over in old airline road route 9 to urinate on the shoulder of the road just before dawn broke a new day.As he was coming up to the calais ,st stephen border crossing he was never so glad to see the canadian flag in his life. Troy crosses the border and drives straight to his mom and dads, they're all gone to work. He jumps in the shower and just stand there for an hour trying to wash away all the bad that night.But even a shower cannot wash away all.Only the blood the precious precious blood of Jesus can wash away all things including the sin of murder.Troy was never charged with that murder,but that gun that he buried in the st stephen new brunswick Canada dirt.Shot and killed that man that night in massachuettes.Troy was very very sad and very very riddled with guilt.He vowed to never ever draw a gun and hurt anyone again as long as he lived.And his body endured a nasty beating because of that promise and commitment.Troy sees his mom and dads house coming up into site.It must be almost 8 months since he has seen or talked to them.

As he grabs the house key from under the welcome mat.As he walks in he sees the old house cat curled up on the couch.His mom and dad are upstairs sleeping.He quietly grabs a pen and paper.Hi mom and dad its Troy i dropped in for a few mins this morning,but you were both still sleeping.i love you both very very much and i'll call you soon .Love Troy.As he leaves the note he wrote on the kitchen table he gently grabs his passport off the top of the fridge. He locks the door and puts the house key back under the welcome mat.Then he walks back down the road to the red rooster to meet up with Paul again.He gently open the door of that freightliner classic truck as to not disturb Paul and he gently pulls it to and sits in the passenger seat.He puts his head back and shuts his eyes.25 minutes later he is awakened by a knock on the door.And he hears a voice dad hey dad are you ready to go?Yes son ill be right up Paul shouts from the sleeper.Paul gets up grabs his heavy insulated jacket and throws it on.Good morning Paul smiles and says to Troy.Do you have to use the restroom or anything asks Paul to Troy? No, I'm good, Troy smiles and says.

Ok i'll be with you in a few mins.as Paul pulls the truck around to fuel it up with diesel he kicks the tires after and checks his straps and lights. As he goes inside to pay his bill.He returns with 2 bottles of orange juice and 2 blueberry muffins.Here you go. Paul smiles and says as he passes a juice and muffin to Troy.Troy reaches out and takes it from Paul and says thank you. Thank

17

you very much for your kindness to me. You are most welcome replies Paul..Paul does up his log book then Troy, Paul and junior hit the road..As they come up to the border Paul sr and Troy cross into the usa first.Good morning guys the customs officer says .Good morning Paul and Troy reply.Going to anderson south carolina today? Asks the customs officer as he looks over Paul's paperwork.Yes sir replies Paul. As he stamps Paul's load manifest he gives a copy back to Paul. He opens Troy's passport then looks at Troy then looks at Troy's picture.Then the customs officer says to Troy.Mr Lewis, what happened to your face?Troy replied i was walking home late one night i took a short cut and feel down and rolled down a steep embankment when i got up this is how i looked. The customs officer scans Troy's passport and says oh that's too bad be careful of a strange area especially at night.Troy smiles and says thank you sir yes i will and i'll try to do much better in the future.Do either of you gentlemen have any drugs, weapons or alcohol on board ? No thay both reply as the customs agent hands Troy's passport back to Paul ,Paul hands it to Troy.Mr Lewis the customs officer says?Yes sir? Replies Troy be careful out there my little boy fell in the dark once and sprained his ankle quite badly.Thank you i will say Troy. You gentlemen have a good safe ride to south carolina. We will say Paul.As Paul and Troy start to head south many many things flooded Troy's mind . I am now officially in the usa. Iam now officially 5 and a half hours from those bad guys in Halifax.He thinks how the $35000 of cocaine will not be forgotten about,even though Troy is not responsible for the missing product All but the $900 he snorted up his nose. Well around 204pm Paul Troy and junior roll onto old exit number 39 off the 495 in dracut massachusetts.

As they go past the cracker barrel restaurant they go 4 or 5 tractor trailer lengths and turn right up a street then an immediate left into the huge office building parking lot,and park their trucks off to the side near the treeline. Paul and junior idle down there trucks for 3 or 4 minutes then shut them off.What are you doing now asks Troy to Paul, Paul smiles and says come with junior and i Troy.We are walking over to the cracker barrel for lunch.No thats ok says Troy i don't have any money i wouldn't want to be a burden.Your no burden replied Paul.No im good thanks says Troy.I like to work and earn my way.Well no problem replies Paul.Climb out of that truck and come over here.Troy gets down and walks over to where Paul is.Paul opens the storage box on the frame of his trailer..He comes back with eight polishing rags a milk crate and something called purple polish california custom.Here ya are Paul smiles and says rub this on my aluminium rims until they turn as dark as the nite ,then take a clean rag and rub it all off!!!What would u like for lunch asks Paul? I pretty much like anything says Troy.They make a killer meatloaf says junior.That would be nice Troy smiles and says. Paul and Junior walk over to the restaurant and Troy goes to work.When Paul and junior return , Troy was working like a little beaver. He had every single rim done on the driver's side of Paul's truck and he just about had the front one on the other side completed. Looks great!!! Paul smiles and says. Finish that up and we will hit the road Ok Troy smiles and says.Paul grabs a couple of clean rags and a small bottle of go jo hand cleaner for Troy.As Troy finishes up and washes his hands,Paul says you did a great job Troy thank you.Your welcome Troy smiles and says.

Here is a nice meatloaf lunch for you sir.Troy cleans his hands and sits in the passenger seat opens up the cellophane box meatloaf with gravy mashed potatoes green beans and roasted carrots Paul inhales a big breath over top of it.Paul chuckles. Good stuff ay buddy?it smells great replies Troy.There's a bottle of water up in the cupboard in the sleeper if u want something to wash it down says Paul. Thanks, Troy.Troy eats his lunch and before you know it their drive time is up and they go to sleep for the night in Sturbridge massachusetts. Thay get up and start there nxt say as the hours and the states pass. At about 4:15am junior and Paul pull into the first rest area After the scales in asheville north carolina .Paul sets his alarm for 620 am

Then he looks over at Troy and asks him hay Troy can you make me up at 620 am buddy if you happen to be awake? Sure says Troy.Troy shuts his eyes in the passenger seat and at 618 like clock work he is wide awake.at 620 am he opens up the curtain and says Paul hey Paul its 620 am my friend

Ugg umm ok Paul says in a groggy voice. As the alarm goes off in the bunk Paul shuts it off and jumps into the driver's seat and stretches .Paul looks over at Troy and says good morning,and thank you for waking me up.Im gonna go

Check my lights and tires and wake junior up.ok says Troy im gonna walk in and use the restroom ok Paul smiles and says so after all that the 3 men get back into the trucks and hit the open road and then just like clockwork.

At 8:53 am they roll into williams building supplies in anderson south carolina

It was a long trip from Halifax Nova Scotia Canada to anderson south carolina usa. As they get out and start to unstrap their load, Troy asks Paul ,Paul how many miles was it to hear anyway? It was 1609 miles my friend Troy smiles and says ..Troy thinks to himself im over 1600 miles away from Halifax and i pray god will help me with my new start.As Troy rolls up the last strap on Pauls load he walks over to juniors load and starts helping him roll up straps. As they get juniors load done Paul says Troy before you leave would it be ok if Junior and I prayed with you?I'd love that Troy smiles and says.they remove their ball caps and pray dear lord please be with this young man help him as he is beginning a new chapter to his life we ask all this in

Jesus name amen. Amen Troy and junior reply.junior opens up his wallet and gives Troy $5 .

I don't want that replies Troy. Ahh just take it says jr payment for helping me and dad. Well thank you Troy smiles and says. As he puts the money into his pocket. As this happens junior says im expecting you to pay me back. What if I never see you again? Ohh you will see me in the kingdom of god if not before.

Well how can i pay you back if i don't see you before the kingdom?Here's how you pay me back junior replies and says remember the kindness shown unto you this day and pass it on to somebody in the future!!! I learned that from my dad, Junior smiles and says!!! I will replies Troy.thay shake hands and Troy walks over to the forklift driver unloading them.excuse me sir do you folks have a restroom i can use.Sure the friendly forklift driver replies.walk in the big overhead door turn right 2nd door on your right pal. Hay thanks a lot, says Troy.

After Troy uses the restroom he washes his hands and face as he is splashing water onto his face he looks in the mirror the swelling of his nose is just about gone and his eye is still pretty black and blue.he drys his hands and face and says a little prayer dear god with your help this is the last time my face will ever look like this but regardless how my face looks ill always smile for you and try to share your love with others for today is the first official day of my new life!!! I pray all this in

Jesus name amen!As he leaves Williams building supplies and begins to walk down the side of the road as he walks about a mile he sees a sign that says 318 county road. He sees another sign that says Oliver's Country store 1 mile.Troy just keeps walking along and he thinks of that old wonderful song again but this time he's smiling ear to ear!!

On a hill far away stood an old rugged cross the emblem of suffering and shame.And i love that old cross where the dearest and best for a world of lost sinners was slain.So ill cherish the old rugged cross till my trophies at last i lay down, i will cling to the old rugged cross and exchange it someday for a crown.maybe he was smiling because he seen the cross on top of the steeple of the anderson community church he walked past .

Or maybe because he felt great about his new start that he was given.Maybe he was smiling because it was a beautiful day outside.But regardless of the reason Troy was smiling ear to ear!! In what seemed to be no time at all Troy made his way right to olivers country store.as he approaches the front porch to enter into the store by what he seen heard and observed,part of it was like going back into time.Almost like a norman rockwell painting and the other part he would sum it up to what seemed to be mass chaos!!! As he walks up the steps 2 enter 2 old men were sitting on the porch at a little table each drinking a can of coca cola and playing checkers.They tip there hats to Troy.Troy nods and

says hello. Then as he walks into the store it seems to be well to put it mildly organised confusion.
A Friendly man stops arguing for a minute looks at Troy and says, howdy with a huge smile on his face!!Troy smiles and says hello.As Troy makes his way to the coolers he sees a bulletin board, and reads a big bold printed ad.And listens to the real friendly man resume his arguing again.Lacey i've told you if they have 3 or more items wrong on the invoice just dont take delivery dear.

Randy how on earth are we gonna keep items on the shelf if we don't take delivery?Lacey last time they said we ordered 7 ice cream sandwich bars.
It was 70 not 7 we sell 7 in a day sometimes dear!!!
UGGGG your impossible

Randy!!! Lacey says in frustration.As all this craziness was ensuing Troy just shakes his head and grins.There was 2 little old ladies that walked up to the cash register and set down a gallon of milk 2 loaves of bread a pint of butterscotch ripple ice cream and a little package of wrigley's spearmint gum.

Oh ,my my lacey what's got you all riled up this morning dear?asks one of the nice old ladys.OH randy is being impossible this morning replies lacey.Oh dear dear don't let that rile you my dear says the little old lady in the pretty green sweater.Yes dear men will be men!! Says the little old lady in the pretty blue dress.Thanks y"all lacey smiles and says.Troy looks over shakes his head a little and just grins again..Ha ha ha ha ha randy chuckles as he pats lacey gently on her shoulder.Good morning ladies.Good morning randy, now you stop getting lacey all upset this morning one of them smiles and says to randy.Lacey is way to nice a person to be in a dither the other one says.Ha ha ha ha randy chuckles God love y"all.That will be $16.48 lacey smiles and says.The lady in the blue dress gives lacey a $20 bill.AND $3.52 is your change thank u very much ladies lacey smiles and says.Lacey bags up there items and hands it to them Y;all have a nice day ladies. Says lacey. Ohh we will.Now randy dont you be giving Lacey a hard time no more today.Ha ha ha ha randy just chuckles.Troy notices a ad and reads it that says hilltop farm requires a farm hand duties will include ,gathering eggs milking cows feeding cows and other livestock and mending fences.Along with other general farm duties.Please apply to person to shirley or randy. Mondays or Tuesdays after 4pm.wensday thursday friday or saturday 9 am to 4pm.address 3850 318 county road.

AfterTroy reads Lacey starts in on randy again.See randy look here we ordered 50 cans of coca cola and they sent us 50.As she unpacks the stock and puts it away.But we ordered 30 moon pies and they sent 3!!!! I think the order packer needs glasses! Troy grins and nods his head again and looks back at the bulletin board again.Ohh lacey dear you're way too young and way too pretty to get so upset it's hard on your blood pressure dear.How many moon pies do we currently have asks randy?There are 10 on the shelf replies lacey.Well now with the 3 thay sent we now have 13 .Ha ha ha ha randy chuckles.Randy today it was four crates of product.I can count a few items but i don't have time to count every single thing.Ha ha ha ha randy chuckles oh Lacey dear don't let it get to you too bad i'm sure we will get it all straight with the good lord's help.Amen to that lacey smiles and says.another guy walks into the store and grabs a chocolate milk and a pop tart. He sets his items on the counter. Good morning Martin Randy says to the man. Good morning he smiles and says.Thats $3.32 please martin.How are you doing randy asks? Just fine martin smiles and says.How are y'all asks martin.Ohh lacey is a little shook up this morning but besides that were all good randy smiles and says. Lacey rolls her eyes.Y'all have a nice day Martin smiles and says. You to Martin lacey replies. Lacey dear i'll call smiths distribution around 11:45 am when the morning rush slows down ok dear?Thankyou Thank you!! Says Lacey to randy.

Troy grabs a .50cent bag of peanuts,and a bottle of lemonade.Randy is out back doing something .Troy walks over to the cash register. Lacey gets up off her knees takes a break from stocking shelves and goes over to the cash register.Good morning says Lacey.Good morning Troy smiles and says.Lacey rings up the peanuts and the lemonade.That's $1.98 will

That be all sugarplum? Lacey smiles and asks? Troy gets the $5 bill out of his pocket that Paul jr gave him and gives it to lacey.Ah yes that's it.he smiles and says. Umm i was reading an ad on your bulletin board ,for hilltop farms, lookin for a farm hand.It says 3850 county road 318.Could you be kind enough to tell me if that's far from here?No not too far, Lacey smiles and says. Just under 2 miles but you won't catch randy or shirley till after 4pm today or tomorrow. Ha ha ha no you wont the store's randy chuckles as he walks by.
Lacey rolls her eyes.Would you happen to know them? Asks Troy.

Yes i do lacey says.Troy looks at the clock on the wall.10 :48 am over 5 hrs Troy says to himself.   Well if i gotta wait 5 hrs i gotta wait no biggie.Troy thinks to himself. I am looking for a job is why i'm inquiring says Troy to the pretty young lady.Im a little hard up for money i'm just kinda anxious to get working.I see lacey smiles and says..A big burly man wearing a plaid shirt comes in and makes his way to the coolers.Randy sticks his head out from the room out back.The guy at the coolers grabs a bottle of 7up and walks up to the counter .good morning lacey 2 hickory smoked bacon breakfast sandwiches for me please lacey.Sure darren Lacey smiles and says.The store's randy says to Troy.Have you ever washed cars b4 young man? I have Troy smiles and says.Have you ever applied wax? Yes, says Troy. I've been busy as a one eyed bear looking for honey randy chuckles and says.The store bought a new ford f150 truck 5 months ago i haven't

27

had a chance to wash it or wax it since i got it. Replied randy.The plaid shirt guy walks up by Troy and waits to be rung up by lacey.Its parked out back replies Randy, meet me there in 5 minutes.I'll get a bucket and soap, a wash mitt and wax and meet ya there ok?

OK, great !!! Troy smiles and says. As Troy walks out behind the store he sees the brand new truck sitting there but from the side door mirrors down it is very very dirty.Troy sets his bottle of lemonade on a crate and eats his peanuts. In afew minutes out comes the stores randy.Ok here are your rags to polish, here's your bucket and soap.Here is a bottle of turtle wax and the garden hose is coiled up around the corner there.Its a 40 ft garden hose so you should have all kinds randy smiles and says.Make her shine and there's a $20 Bill in it for ya says randy.Hey mr thanks thanks alot!! Troy smiles and says.

I sure can use the extra money!!! No problem no problem, Randy smiles and says!!! Ok thank you sir.Troy rolls up his sleeves and gets to work.
At 1245 pm Lacey comes out with 2 slices of pepperoni pizza and a can of coke for Troy. We have a lunch special says lacey 2 slices and a coke for $4.00 replied lacey.I can't pay for it says Troy i don't have enough money.You just enjoy It sugar plum replies lacey it on the store.

He now has the truck completely washed and the wax applied and removed on the front drivers fender and drivers door.Thank you replies Troy to lacey.
As he sits down to eat his lunch he says grace and then looks up into the sky and says god even though i don't deserve it you have shown me great grace and kindness. Thank you father! And I mean it!!! I'm gonna live for you for the rest of my days! Troy takes a bite of the delicious pepperoni pizza!!! And looks over at the logo on the f150 door."olivers country store" that's a nice logo he thinks to himself.He takes a big drink of his can of coke and thinks how good his food and drink taste after working hard on this truck.He finishes his lunch and goes back to work. He works away and has it looking real good .About an hour later he goes into the store.he finds randy and says i have it all done would u ,ike to come take a look at it?Sure ill be right out says randy.Randy comes out and looks it over.Looks great young man reaches into his pocket and pulls out a $20 bill as he promised and hands it to Troy.I coiled the hose all back up. Where would u like the soap wax and wash mitt? Just leave it by the back entrance young man. I'll put it away later.Troy does what Randy asks and goes into the store Thanks a bunch . Randy chuckles no problem young man thank you. Troy starts to walk towards hilltop farm. He gets there and looks at his watch its 3;29 pm and he thinks to himself this randy and shirley should be here in 31 minutes.should be around.he leans against a tall fence posts by the sign that says hilltop farm. At 357 pm a pretty middle aged lady pulls in with a grey crown victoria.She stops

and says to Troy.Hi young man can i help you with
something? Yes please im looking for randy or shirley.
 I'm interested in the farm hand job.
Well im shirley randy should be home any minute. Walk
on up to the house and I'll fix us a glass of sweet tea.

Thanks, Troy smiles and says Shirley drives her crown
victoria up the driveway. Troy makes his way up
walking.As Troy sits down on the beautiful front porch
At the farmhouse,Shirley comes out with 2 tall glasses
of sweet tea filled with ice cubes!!!Thank you so much
Troy smiles and says. SO you're interested in
 The farm hand job? Oh very much so Troy replies. As
there talking up through the drive comes a shiny f150
ford truck.With olivers country store written on the door.
Oh here's Randy now, Shirley smiles and says. Troy
giggles so let me guess randy is your husband? Thats
right says shirley.Do you know him? Oh yes I do replies
Troy but I haven't know him for long.Well howdy Randy
says to Shirley and Troy.Hi hun Shirley smiles and
says.You said you knew randy a short time? Asks
shirley to Troy.OH where are my manners ? We didn't
introduce ourselves im shirley and this is my husband
randy.Let me guess Troy

Interrupt and say's let me guess oliver?Yep shirley
smiles and says. You said you knew Randy for a short
time?. .Yes, replied Troy from this morning , when we
met. Hay hun look out at the new truck.It looks great

dear did you take it to Johnson's car wash and detailing in town?Troy sips away on his sweet tea.

No, that young man sitting right there did it. Replied randy. Shirley, you conduct the rest of this interview say's Randy. I've seen his work. I'm going for a nap! Troy extends his hand to Shirley and smiles. I'm Troy Troy Lewis . i'm Shirley Shirley oliver. Have you ever worked as a farm hand b4? Asks shirley?

No mame says Troy but im honest and reliable and im very very hard working!! Well says shirley the job will consist of early morning and late afternoon milking of cows .Chicken feeding crop planting weeding watering And harvesting of crops. Cleaning stables. Have you ever operated a farm tractor before?No mame but I'm willing to learn. And when i was younger i operated a wood skidder up north from where i come from it's a machine that takes the logs out of the woods so i'm sure they are similar.Ok shirley smiles and replies.Well the job includes room and board and pays $7.00 per hour. That's great!!! Troy smiles and says. I'd love to have it!!!! Shirley sticks out her hand and shakes Troy's hand. You're hired. Welcome to hilltop farm.Troy smiles widely thank you thank you so much. Your check will be ready at 2pm every Friday and if you wanna use one of the farm trucks to run in town to cash it on friday that's no problem. And sunday will be your day off.Randy gets up at 430 am on sunday and does the early morning milking.A nd i handle the milking at suppertime sunday afternoon.By us all working together we get it done and you get a day off and we all can get to church.

Where do you go to church? Asks Troy? We go to the anderson community church up the road.Oh very nice replies Troy. I'd be happy to attend with you folks on sundays!!Troy thinks to himself how he hasn't been to church in so long , but when God is opening doors for him he feels it's time to open the door to church and start to attend faithfully.

Well shirley says lets show you to your room .Oh by the way says shirley don't you have a suitcase or anything?No mame everything i have is in my pockets And I own an old toyota car but that is at my cousins house over in maine. I am ashamed to admit it. But i have made a lot of poor decisions in my life,
But with this nice new job you and God have given me, I pray I'm off to a great new start!!!Shirley smiles and looks at the young man and says:"if my people which are called by my name shall humble themselves and pray, and seek my face, and turn from their wicked ways, then will i hear from heaven and will forgive their sin, and will heal their land. . 2nd chronicles 7:14.
That's beautiful replies Troy!! My grandma used to read the bible to me at the end of every day when I was little and stayed with her. Shirley smiles and says your about the size of my son craig let me look in his old room im sure he left some clothes he didn't take away to college with him.Shirley takes Troy into his room.It has a double

bed   radio, a chair and a desk. And on top of that desk sits a king james version bible Troy thinks to himself i'll be reading this everyday! Time to develop some good habits. Off in the corner there is a small bathroom with a stand up shower a sink and a toilet. This is perfect, thinks Troy.shirley sticks her head around the corner. Troy let me check something real quick dear.Yep ok there is great. There is lots of soap and shampoo whenever u wanna take a shower and there's 3 towels on top of the medicine cabinet too. Now to go check on those clothes in craig's room.Shirley returns with a pair of pyjama bottoms and a pair of swimming trunks1 sweater a pair of black cotton pants a pair of jeans a blue t shirt a package of new underwear and a new package of socks. Hear you go!!! Aww thanks so much mame. Replied Troy. Please don't call me mame. It makes me feel old, call me shirley.You got it shirley Troy smiles and says!!! Well i'm gonna go fix supper says shirley it's ready every night at 530pm.Breakfast is 730 am sharp every morning and lunch is 1230 pm every day except mondays and tuesdays because randy is at the store and i'm nursing at the old folks home.So on those days you will just have to fend for yourself and make a grill cheese or something ok? Ok thanks shirley says Troy. Shirley says welcome, make yourself comfortable. Shirley goes down to fix supper Troy gets in his shower and takes a nice warm shower.It feels so good cause he hasn't had one for about 5 days. He has quite a scruff growing he thinks to himself i'll ask randy if he has an extra disposable razor after supper. He looks at his watch its 448 pm. He sees the old king

James laying on the desk he grabs it and opens it up to read it. He sits on his bed as he opens it up he sees a note inside it says To whatever souls is using this room. Your friends randy and shirley oliver. Troy bows his head and says GOD it's been so long since i've read your holy word Please help me to grow and learn in Jesus name amen. He opens it up to psalms 88 and begins to read Lord god of my salvation i have cried day and night before thee. Let my prayer come before thee Incline thine ear unto my cry, for my soul is full of troubles.

Troy reads right up to Psalms 104 verse 24 O lord how manifold are thy works In wisdom thou made them all.

He hears a knock on his door. Come on in, he says. Randy is grinning as he opens the door.

Are you hungry young man?
Yes very replies Troy
Well come on down and get it!! Ohh and by the way if i was you I'd pick up that book and read it everyday . I am going to. Troy smiles and says.

Troy goes down stairs and enjoys a wonderful supper with Randy and Shirley, a supper of Caesar salad, baked potatoes and carrots and pork chops and for dessert pecan pie and vanilla ice cream on top.
Thank you so much Shirley and Randy. That was delicious. Your welcome Shirley smiles and says . Troy

gets up, clears his dishes to the sink and clears randys and shirleys to the sink too. Thank you young man replied randy

My pleasure Troy smiles and says.

Shirley, would you like a hand with the dishes? Troy asks

No Troy that's fine but thanks for asking, says shirley. No problem replies Troy.Hay randy would you have disposable razor and a little can of shave cream i could have? I just picked some up the other day

Randy smiles and replies i'll go get them for you. Thanks says Troy.

Randy goes into the washroom and returns with 2 disposable razors and a small can of shave creme. This can is about half empty replies randy but i think it will take care of the scruff on your face he smiles and says. What time would you folks like me start in the morning, asks Troy?

IS 430 am ok with you? Asks randy. Yes, replied Troy. I'm gonna go shave and turn in for a good night's sleep 430 am comes early . i'll go out with ya and give ya a crash course in the morning. Thanks so much replied Troy your welcome says randy. Hey Troy come here please. Shirley takes Randy's hand and Troys and says let's bow our heads and pray. Dear lord Jesus thank you so much for sending this young man to us to help with our farm let him feel at home here be with him everyday show him your love everyday .in Jesus name amen.amen says randy..Amen replied Troy. Troy are you ok? Asks shirley

Oh yes replied Troy.As we were praying my mind just went to my grandma she always prayed with me when i was little as Troy wipes a tear off his face.
Randy smiles and says it sounds like God blessed you with a great grandma . yes he did replied Troy lately i've been thinking of her often.That's God says shirley.
And now God continues to bless me with my great 2 new friends Randy and shirley. Aww bless your heart says shirley goodnite Troy says as he walks upstairs.
Goodnite replied Randy and shirley.

Troy goes into his bedroom after he shaves he kneels down to pray. Dear lord
Thank you so much for this new start you have given me. I am sure there will be challenges and obstacles as i go through my daily life, but I'm asking you to help me and no matter how hard it may get from time to time help me to always keep my focus on you. In Jesus name amen.

Chapter 3 Troy makes a new friend

As Troy settles into his new role, Shirley says to him one afternoon.

Troy you are a natural , you are catching on just fine!! Thank you. Troy smiles and says what time are you folks leaving for church in the morning? We are leaving at 1015 am sharp. It's a 5 minute drive and church starts at 1030am.Would it be ok if I got a ride to church with you and Randy on Sunday asks Troy? Sure dear, that would be fine. As shirley and Troy

Finish up the farm work for the day,Troy gets up at up at 8am On Sunday morning. He shaves and brushes his teeth He puts on his best shirt that he has and a pair of black cotton pants.

He prays a little prayer as he gets dressed.Lord i haven't been to church in alot of years. But with your help I'm putting the bad things I have done behind me,and my best foot forward to love and serve you lord.For the rest of my days. In Jesus name amen.As he goes down into the kitchen he notices randys and shirley's door is partially open, he looks in they are sound asleep

He smiles as he walks past.He goes into the kitchen grabs the eggs bacon   fry pan and brews some coffee. He sings an old song that is familiar to him.One from his childhood.

Then sings my soul my saviour god to thee how great thou art how great thou art.Good morning randy interrupts and says Hope you made some scrambled eggs that's shirley's favourite. Please please continue with your singing. I love that old hymn, says randy. Troy smiles..Troy starts singing again.Then sings my soul my saviour god to thee.

Oh that's music to my ears, Shirley smiles and says.!! And those eggs are delicious by the way.Troy looks up and smiles. As Troy serves breakfast, Randy and Shirley sit down .What a beautiful breakfast Randy smiles and says.

Well thank you Troy smiles and says.After they all get their stomachs full Randy looks at his watch 947 am well i'm gonna brush my teeth says randy
It's a beautiful morning. I'm gonna sit on the front porch and read my bible, says shirley. You guys go ahead i'll clean up replied Troy.Ok thanks Troy says shirley.
Well after some sudsy water a rinse and a dry Troy looks at the clock 1011 am aww perfect timing he thinks

to himself.. Time to wash my hands, grab my bible then off to church.. As shirley Troy and randy get in the car when they pull into the church yard in anderson community church it is 1021 am

As Shirley Randy and Troy walk into church they are greeted by a friendly pastor's voice. Good morning Mr and Mrs oliver. Good morning they smile and say.Pastor tom extends his hand to Troy and asks the olivers and who is this young man you have with you this morning? Pastor this is Troy ,Troy Lewis our new farm hand.Troy smiles and extends his hand. It's nice to meet you, pastor tom says Troy.

The pleasure is all mine. And you are in for a special treat today to says pastor tom to Troy. Really? Asks Troy. Oh yes, replies pastor Tom .We have a missionary from Finland this morning who is our main speaker,A nd special music from the Sunday school choir and a lovely young lady who attends our church. Well that sounds wonderful, Troy says.

As pastor tom is telling Troy all this a beautiful blond haired blue eyed girl in a Red dress stops and talks to shirley. Then she says good morning pastor tom and shakes his hand and says good morning to randy. Troy thinks i know this lady she stops looks at Troy and says good morning sugar plum so nice to see you in the house of the lord this morning.Good morning lacy i'm glad to be here Troy smiles and says.And lacey is part of our special music this morning says pastor tom. Well

I am really looking forward to it.says Troy. Well let's all get a seat, says randy. As they sit down Randy looks over at Troy and says wait till you hear her sing.Voice of an angel says shirley.Randy says to Troy and shirley that's why i hate to see her get so shook up at the store over things.

What do you mean?asks Troy.Randy says well you know it drives up her blood pressure she is such a sweet girl, so greatly used of god replies randy i just hate to see her

Get so upset.Yes i noticed she takes the order accuracy to heart replies Troy.

Oh you guys she's young and strong, says shirley.Still i don't like it, says randy.

Good morning everyone says pastor tom to the congregation.It's nice to see you all in the house of the lord this morning.We have a wonderful service this morning. Brother and sister david and monique trennelson missionaries to finland are with us this morning.They have a message for us and a report from finland and the great things god is doing there.And also lacey jones will be doing 2 musical numbers this morning and the anderson community church Sunday school choir will be performing today as well.Let's bow our heads and pray.As Troy bows his head and prays he is smiling ear to ear.Then i think it's fair to say the peace of god, the peace that passes all understanding swept over him.As he prays he thinks to himself,Lord i promised to serve you the rest of my life.I feel so at home hear. Thank you lord for placing me here.

Thank you lord for your love to me and your love for all of us.As he finishes praying he hears pastor tom ending his prayer.And lord we ask all this in Jesus name amen..and the congregation all says amen.Ladies and gentlemen the anderson community church sunday school choir.Everyone applauds loudly and 15 precious little souls take the stage ranging in age from 7 to 14. Thay preform this is the day that the lord has made and i got the love of Jesus

In my heart.As the choir is smiling if roars of applause after their number, Troy thinks to himself Lord this is wonderful!!!I can feel you speaking to me through the words of the childrens songs.One of the choir members steps forward all alone and says lacey will you please do us the honour of singing our 3rd and final song with us?Lacey smiles big and bright from the 5th row back on the right hand side and says i'd be happy to and it's my honour to perform with all of you! As she takes the stage she says to the choir and what song are we gonna sing for everyone this morning?How about Jesus loves me, one little girl says to lacey. That's a wonderful song replied lacey.As lacey belts out the opening line Troy is just smiling ear to ear he thinks he's crash landed in heaven and he's hearing an angels voice.Jesus loves me this i know for the bible tells me so little ones to him belong they are weak but he is strong .Yes Jesus loves me yes Jesus loves me yes Jesus loves me the bible tells me so.

Now the whole choir joins in with lacey. Yes Jesus loves me yes Jesus loves me yes Jesus loves me the bible tells me so.AS lacey starts chorus number 2
Tears of joy are falling down Troys face. Maybe this is where i went wrong and yet where i'm making it right again. By forgetting and remembering these words Troy says Troy to himself.Shirley notices Troy crying and she gently taps Randy's forearm . Randy nods and smiles. And grasps shirley's hand.

If there were ever 2 saints of god that helped the weary weak and downtrodden it was randy and shirley oliver!! As Lacey and the Sunday school choir finish up the congregation erupts with applause. Let's hear it for the Anderson community church Sunday school choir lacey smiles and says.

All the kids exit to the right of the platform.Lacey smiles and says they were great werent they?This morning I'd like to do an oldie but it's goodie for y'all says lacey. It's one of my all time favourites. The old rugged cross. On a hill far away stood an old rugged cross the emblem of suffering and shame. And I love that old cross where the dearest and best for a world of lost sinners was slain. As Lacey sings this beautiful old gospel song.Troys tears have stopped flowing from his eyes but his smile has not subsided one bit!!!!

AS lacey sings Troy's mind goes to many places ,he thinks to the nite he got Beat up very badly in Halifax Nova Scotia. He thinks of being 10 and sitting in church with his grandma and hearing this beautiful beautiful song!! He thinks of the kindness that Paul and junior showed him! And most importantly he thinks of God how he is the god of 2nd chances!!! And how he's not willing that any should perish but that all should come to repentance. And how he is rich in mercy and love!!! Just like the holy word says in Ephesians chapter 2 verses 4 ,5 and 6.And his mind slips back to the song Lacey is singing!!

Troy is happy as he can be!!!Lacey finishes and god's house erupted with applause!!!

The missionary from Finland comes and speaks to the congregation. The whole service was just a wonderful service and it seemed to fly by.

After church pastor tom and brother and sister david and monique are shaking the parishioners hands.As Troy makes his way out pastor tom shakes his hand and says to him it was so nice to have you young man.Troy smiles and says thank you so much i'll definitely be back! That's wonderful replies pastor tom.. As Troy makes his way out to the parking lot he sees Lacey standing there.

Umm excuse me lacey right? He says as he walks up to her..Yes lacey

Smiled and replied. We both work for randy Troy says you at the store and me at the farm.Hey sugar plum! Lacey replies.I just wanted to let you know your singing today was wonderful!!! Replies Troy.Aww thanks sugar plum

So very kind of you but im nothing without the lord. OH for sure replies Troy.It's like me lacey i have made poor decisions and bad very bad mistakes sometimes,But i know God has always looked out for me, I know God has forgiven me!! Lacey smiles big and bright and beautiful!!!! Well that's wonderful sugar plum!!!

Troy notices out of the corner of his eye on the beautiful beautiful day

That randy and shirley are standing around talking to people.

All of a sudden lacey says to him.Sugar plum do you have any plans for lunch? No, Troy, nothing planned.Lacey smiles and says every sunday i always take my grandma to my house and fix lunch with her and have a little visit with her you know? Well that sounds just wonderful .replied Troy.

Well why don't you join us lacey smiles and says? I'd be happy to say,s Troy.Thats my car down there in the corner the little red one grandma and i will be there waiting for you, after you notify randy and shirley? Notify ? asks Troy.

Well yes sugar plum you're gonna tell them you're going to my house so that they won't be worried about you arent you? Oh yes yes replied Troy Sorry i had a brain freeze. It's all good sugar plum lacey smiles and says..As lacey walks to her car Troy walks over to randy and shirley.Troy tells them about laceys lunch invitation they say ok no problem.Troy walks over to laceys car and gets in the back seat. Sugar plum, why are you getting in the back seat?

Well your grandma replied Troy . won't she be coming out of church soon?Oh grandma goes to church with me every morning replies lacey but this morning she had a bad headache so she stayed home. Ohh I'm sorry to hear that. Thanks says lacey so you may as well jump right up front with me because she spent the night at my house last night.Oh ok Troy smiles and says.Lacey and Troy have a wonderful drive and chat from the church to lacey's house .They shut the car off and go on inside.As they go inside ,,

Laceys grandma is standing at the counter mixing up a fresh pitcher of lemonade. Hi grandma how are you feeling asks lacey?Grandma looks over at lacey fine child fine.

My headache is all gone.And who is this nice young man with you lacey? Hi i'm Troy Troy Lewis its very nice to meet you.Troy extends his hand to grandma she shakes it well hi young man it's great to meet you im laceys grandma rhonda jones.Hi miss jones it's a pleasure replies Troy.

You young man replies rhonda .well how does grilled cheese potato salad lemonade and chocolate ice cream for dessert sound for lunch?

Sounds wonderful, replies Troy. Well thanks sugar plum lacey smiles and says.Troy, rhonda and lacey have a wonderful lunch and share some laughs.

After dessert rhonda says you kids excuse me im gonna go call my friends stephanie and megan , see if there gonna go to the coffee shop this

afternoon.If they are, I'm gonna join them. As Rhonda turns to go into the living room. Troy says it was very nice to meet you rhonda.Rhonda walks over

Troy gives her a big hug and says God bless you young man.

Lacey is smiling,while this is taking place. God bless you to   replies Troy..Rhonda looks over at lacey.Lacey? Yes grandma. He's a good one.

Lacey just grins.Lacey and Troy clean off the kitchen table and do up

The lunch dishes.Stephanie and Megan pull into the drive to pick up rhonda.Rhonda gets into the car and the girls take off.Then lacey says to Troy. Feel like taking a walk before I take you back to Randy and shirleys? Well that sounds great ! Troy smiles and says.As lacey and Troy walk and talk the nxt thing you know the afternoon flew right past.Lacey looks down at her watch

Its 449 pm. I better get you back home. Yes, I got a 4am start in the morning for milking.. I'm going into the store for 5am for stocking ill stock

Till 550am then we open up for 6 am and the morning rush begins.

Lacey i wanna thank you for the wonderful lunch and the even more wonderful afternoon!!Lacey smiles its my pleasure, thank you for coming!!!

As they round the corner and walk up laceys drive lacey goes in the house and grabs her car keys hop in Troy ill take ya home.

They drive and talk till no time flat. They are at Shirley and randys.

Thanks again for a lovely afternoon says Troy.He grabs the door handle and opens up his door.Hey sugar plum? Yes? Replies Troy.Are you coming to bible study wednesday night ? asks lacey.What time does it start?7pm replied lacey.I wouldn't miss it for the world says Troy as he exits the car.Hay sugar plum come over to my door for a minute. Troy walks over and sticks his head in the window, yes lacey he asks? I'll pick you up here at 645 pm sharp ok?

Ok that sounds great, Troy smiles and says. Lacey quickly plants a little kiss on Troy's cheek. Troy smiles and steps back, Lacey smiles and backs down the drive. It had been a long time since anyone had expressed any romantic interest in Troy.As Troy is standing there holding his cheek Lacey pulls the car into drive, starts down the road and gives a little honk. Troy smiles and waves still holding his cheek.Troy thinks to himself of a new start but never in a million years did he dream it would be such a wonderful new start!But us humans we all tend to forget from time to time, that with God all things are possible!!!!!

Frederick Demerchant

Chapter 4   400am question period.

Good morning good morning says randy as he is walking into the barn at 408 am.Good morning Troy smiles brightly and says!!!How are you this morning?Oh I'm just great replies randy just great.Randy i just wanna thank you and Shirley once again for all the kindness you folks have shown unto me!!Oh it's our pleasure!!And we both appreciate all the hard work you have been doing around here!! Oh randy you don't know how refreshing and how much of a stress reliever me working on this farm has been for me.

Well I'm glad Troy.replied randy. Where shirley and i are getting older all help is always greatly appreciated!!! But just think Troy one day when we get to our new home in heaven the lords gonna give us all a new body where we will never grow old!!!Ya Troy smiles and says and no more getting up for 4am milkings!! Both randy and Troy share a chuckle!! So umm randy what is the deal with lacey?Asks Troy.Ha ha ha ha ha lacey she's a livewire! Randy smiles and says.But a great girl, and she loves the lord! I love her like shes my own daughter says randy.Dont i know it says Troy and she is a wonderful singer to!!

Yes she can really belt it out says randy.How old is lacey randy? Asks Troy.How old do you think she is asks randy?well id say shes about 27 or 28 says

Troy.Well your pretty far off says randy.Iam asks Troy yes you are.

She turned 32 on her last birthday on sept 17th.really ? I never would have guessed she was that old, says Troy she sure doesn't look it.

Was she ever married ?asks Troy Troy to randy? Yes, a long long time ago, replied randy. See lacey has always been a go getter i've know her since she was 5 days old when her mama used to bring her into the store.She graduated at the age of 18 at the top of her class out of a graduating class of 48.Wow thats mighty impressive replied Troy!Yes , says randy.She enlisted in the united states air force and served her country for 2 yrs.At the age of 20 she got an honourable discharge.It was while she was in the air force she met her husband barry.Barry was four years older than lacey says randy. Like lacey he joined the airforce right out of high school as well.

And he rose to the rank of master corporal in just 4 yrs.2 months after lacey got her honourable discharge lacey and barry gor married.Barry remained enlisted as an aircraft mechanic and lacey went to work as a secretary for the welding shop here in town.4 months after their marriage barry was driving home on leave to anderson here from up north in stumpy point north carolina air force base where he was stationed.He was just 35 miles from home and a drunk driver crossed the line and hit barry head on!!! Oh no that's awful! says Troy.Barry died instantly. Very very sad says Troy.Yes it sure was says randy. The other man lived but he endured 3 major surgeries and about 1 yr of physical rehab afterward.About the only good thing that came out of that accident was he never drank again and he gave his heart to the lord. Well Lacey just threw herself into her work and her family, that was her way of coping and dealing with it.What a sad tragic thing for a new young bride to have to go through, replied Troy.Yes says randy this is why i hate to see her get all upset if our delivery inventory order isn't right. .It raises her blood pressure and it isn't good for her. Well randy when did lacey come to work for you at the store ? this upcoming january lacey has worked for me for 7 years.Wow a long time says Troy. Yes she worked at a golf course for a summer mowing grass and stuff like that after the secretary job at the welding shop got laid off from that 1 week before Christmas, enjoyed her holidays started with me january 3rd and has been there ever since.

Wow she has been a dedicated employee for you.Everybody loves Lacey including Shirley and i, she just gives off that feel or flow you know that when you're around her it just brightens your day!!! Well that's awesome!!!

Well, has she had any boyfriends after barry? Ha ha ha ha funny you should ask, says randy she went out with steve henley for about 45 days. Ha ha ha ha randy chuckles.Well 2 ques randy why are u chuckling and who is steve henley? Well Steve henley has always had trouble since he was about 2 years old.Oh really? Asks Troy . He always starts off as nice and polite and treating women right . but it dont take long for his true colours to come out.

Lacey told me she had started dating him and they went out 2 or 3 times. I said oh lacey dear lacey lacey i don't mean to pry but he's not a very nice man .I don't mean to pry but i think this is a bad idea. Lacey just giggled and said oh randy dont worry he's not like that anymore and he promised me he's gonna start going to church with me on sundays.Well did he ever go to church with her? Ya a sunday or 2 replied randy . One nite lacey was scheduled to work at the store till 8 pm he came in about 802 pm and starts streaming at her asking if she knew how to tell time? I spoke up and said young man we don't talk to people that way in this store. He looked at me and said who are you to talk to me ? I'll speak to anyone anyway I want.

Well i got mad Troy i said im randy oliver the owner of this store and you will not talk to lacey or anyone else this way in this store. Well he said to me well come on rate outside and i'll box your ears and then we will talk about it!!

Lacey starts yelling Steve stop it so i came out from behind the counter and steves going outside lucky we didn't have any customers at the time lacey runs outside quickly and says steve now stop it stop it i'll be right out.

Well all of a sudden he hit poor little lacey he slapped her right across the face. Well, I was just coming through the door when this happened and it happened in front of Steve's car , which is parked about

35 feet from the door. Oh no that's horrible, says Troy!!! Well i start to run cause as i said i love lacey like one of my own kids.Now im no the man but i had every intention of grabbing him by his throat and giving him a little squeeze to open his car door and run him out of there !!! I don't blame you a bit Troy replied!!

So i start to run over there and Troy im telling you before i got 8 ft from the hood of that car lacey had steve on the ground with his wrist bent over and his arm halfway up his back he was letting the kye eyes out of him let me tell ya!!! Ha ha ha ha randy chuckles.That clown messed with the wrong lady let me tell you!! Wow replies Troy.Remember i told you earlier that lacey was a go getter? Well unbeknownst to any of us lacey had studied karate in the airforce! Needless to say that was the end of lacey and steve. He doesn't come to the store anymore. You know one thing i'm realizing now that i've totally rededicated my life to the lord randy? What's that Troy? Well this is why sin is so horrible sometimes we get drug so far down in sin we don't even totally realise what sin is doing to us! Amen to that randy smiles and says.

Living for the lord is the best way! Says Troy. Randy places his hand on Troy's shoulder.Troy I want you to know I'm very very proud of you.

Now tell me why all these questions about lacey? Well randy i Had a lovely afternoon with lacey yesterday. And she even gave me kiss on the cheek when she dropped me off yesterday. Ah ah ah ah ithink love might be brewing in the air randy smiles and says.Well she seems to be a lovely lovely girl replies

Troy. Let me tell you something Troy .If I was you i'd think it over and see where it goes.Lacey is a wonderful person. Do you know what i think randy? What's that Troy . I think her getting to work around you alot and seeing the wonderful Christian man you are is rubbing off on her.

Aww how very very kind if you Troy!! Well its true randy. You know randy

I feel the holy spirit is leading me to tell you something and I hope you don't think less of me for what I am about to tell you. But for a lot of years i was running drugs from Canada where i grew up to down into boston massachusetts and at first it was strictly for money when i was a very very young man i used to do logging out in the forest cutting down trees and taking the skidder and taking them to the laydown yard to be loaded onto trucks to go to mills to be processed .Well when that industry died off in new brunswick and i got laid off,i could make more money on one run which took 26 to 27 hrs to com

plete then i could make at logging for a week.And i made a living at logging.some weeks id do 2 or even 3 runs.But you know it was wrong randy

It was wrong of me to do.When i was 29 years old i had a new ford half ton truck and i bought a great little house and paid cash for it and had over

$9800 cash in a shoe box buried at the edge of my property.

But I got caught up in it you know.I lost it all. I took my eyes off of Christ and followed after sin and trust me, I've paid a very very heavy price.

Troy let go of that udder and come over here for a minute, replied randy.

Randy takes the little new testament out of his breast pocket

I want you to read 3 scriptures this morning ok? Ok replied Troy.

Randy thumbs through the pages of his little new testament.Ahh yes here is the first one, Troy read Romans 3 vs 23 and 24.

Troy picks up the book and begins to read aloud

For all have sinned and come short of the glory of god.Being justified

Freely by his grace through the redemption that is in Christ Jesus.

Now flip that little jewel to 1st john 2 vs 1.

Troy flips through the little pages till he finds it.Ahh here it is randy.

Read aloud Troy, randy smiles and says. My little children, these things I write unto you that ye sin not.And if any man sin, we have an advocate with the father ,Jesus Christ the righteous.

Remember that Troy as Randy gently puts his hand on his shoulder. Remember that. And no matter what no matter how far down you may have fallen you have an advocate with the father.Jesus.

Thank you randy i will see when i was younger i didn't have any spiritual

Guidance well except for my grandma when i was a kid.

Thats why im so glad god placed me here with you dear sweet folks

Replies Troy. I feel I'm exactly where God wants me to be, and I feel I am exactly with who he wants me to be with. And the kindness and love you and Shirley have shown me is phenomenal!! And I just want to say thank you from the bottom of my heart!!! Well you know shirley and i just try to be as much like Jesus as we possibly can.Now i have a now i have a question for you.

Sure replies Troy. Did you know that the first time you walked into my store I could tell that you were a soul seeking for more of god?

Really replied Troy? Yes really.How could you randy? Well i'm not really sure but it's just a god given talent the lord has bestowed on me i guess.

And also you walk and talk and carry yourself in a polite humble way.

My experience has been most people that conduct themselves this way

Has had an experience with the holy spirit. Remember Troy were saved

By grace but sanctified throughout a lifetime.I've never thought of it that way before randy, but it makes sense doesn't it. .Yes it does thank god for his patience ,grace, mercy and love!!! Now let's get this milking done and you can go in and scramble some eggs and butter some toast. Sounds great randy

After the milking is complete and randy shirley and Troy share a hearty breakfast as Troy goes on with his day he thinks about what him and randy talked about he thinks of Christ and his love and sacrifice for humanity and he thinks of lacey.Well it's now about 1112 am and randy and lacey are working away at the store together. The morning rush has now slowed and the lunch rush hasn't started yet.Lacey dear says randy .Yes randy replied lacey there was a certain young man in my barn this morning about 420 am asking a lot of questions about you.There was replied lacey? There sure was, Randy says.

Lacey giggles.Troy is a nice young man. How is he catching on to farming? Lacey, you know he's doing great at it!! He's a great worker who never ever complains.and he does his work very thoroughly.

Well that sounds lovely.says lacey. You know Troy and I had a good talk about the lord to lacey. Oh that's nice, says lacey , we had a nice walk and talk Sunday as well. I think he is searching more and more for a deeper relationship with God. What do you think randy? I would agree with you lacey. Can you remember what Jesus said on the sermon on Mount lacey? I sure can lacey smiles and say blessed are they which hunger and thirst after righteousness for they shall be filled. That's right, Randy says. Troys going to bible study with me wednesday night!!! You know that's the type of man and the only type of man I'm interested in is one that loves god!! I think you are wise beyond your years to think that way lacey!!Ya i thought i could change steve

But that didn't work.ha ha ha ha randy laughs ya i told him about the

Fiasco we had here at the store with him.Ohhhh no randy you didn't. Ohhh ya i did say,s randy.I remember that night so vividly says lacey. I just wish i could have gotten outside sooner, ahh randy how sweet of you but the old martial arts training kicked in!!!

Ha ha ha ha taught that guy a lesson he won't soon forget!!replied randy.

I really like Troy alot says lacey. That's wonderful ,well just take it day by day and see what God does. Thanks randy. You're welcome dear.

As one day goes on eventually it ends. And tomorrow is a new day.

Chapter 5 " a stranger comes to town"

That sure was a great bible study tonight lacey.Yes for sure im so proud of you its your 3rd in a row? Yes it is, I really like them replied Troy.

Aww thats great replied lacey.Troy gets into laceys car and she takes him home like any other wednesday night.Last wednesday Troy officially asked lacey to be his

Girlfriend and she said yes as lacey drops off Troy randy is out by the barn and sees them pull up.Troy did happen to see a black Lincoln anywhere on the road? No i don't believe i did replies Troy.Well he was here earlier asking lots of questions about who works on this farm and stuff i asked him why he wanted to know he thanked me for my time and left.Did he seem to

Have any outstanding characteristics randy? Well not really but he seemed to have a northern accent to me.What was he dressed like asks Troy?

Well he had on brown cotton pants and a green and white flannel shirt id say he was probably around 38 to 41 yrs old.

Now the 2 men that jumped Troy in the restroom in Massachusetts were around that age.Troy immediately got a bad bad feeling deep down in the pit of his stomach.Troy are you ok ask randy? Umm what replied Troy? A million and one things were flowing

through Troys mind rate now.They would never find him all the way down here would thay?Or was the drug lords in kahoots,
with the United States customs at calais? He was doing so good at his new start.You reap what you sow .Was it a contract killer come to do Troy in?

Troy knew the best thing he could do ,the absolute best thing he could do is get on his knees and pray about it to the lord.Troy ? Troy? Umm ya ya sorry randy i just got something on my mind.Im sorry i apologize.Son are you alright randy lovingly asks.Yes, yes randy just fine.Im just a little tired and 4 am comes early .I didn't see a black lincoln but if i do i'll let you know.im gonna turn in.Troy makes his way towards the house.Hay Troy shouts randy.Yes randy answers Troy.Im here if you need to talk.Thanks randy replied Troy. Troy goes into the kitchen and pours a big glass of milk he chugs it down in 4 gulps.

Then he goes into his bedroom and begins to pray.Dear Lord, you know

I have rededicated my life to you. And you know that I love you.I am going to continue to follow you until my last day and my last breath. I don't know who this guy is that came around here asking randy questions.

And i also don't know if anyone from my former life knows i'm here but I love you God. And i pray no matter what is going on you will help me and protect me and guide me in the things you want me to say.Give me the words to say at the proper time and in the right context.Keep me in your loving care   god.I ask all this in Jesus name amen.Troys prayer must have helped to

Put his mind at ease for he slept like a baby.As he is working away at 417am he is startled, for very very quickly comes a loud knock on the man door.He jumps to his feet very very quickly and grabs a piece of 2 ft steel rebar over in the corner .The bang on the door this time is louder Troy stands about 7 ft off to the side of the door and says in a loud voice.Ya who is it?

The voice says im looking for Troy Lewis may i come in ? Who are you?Says Troy. My name is carl.Carl tozer im a united states federal marshall and im looking for mr Troy andrew Lewis .And i was told i may be able to find him here.Troys middle name was andrew besides how many people would be looking for someone at 417 am.Sir do you have a badge? Yes i do ,replies the officer. Please slowly open the door and show it to me.The officer does as he is asked Troy says come in .Troy walks over to the nearest little corner shelf and sets the rebar on it.Officer carl watches him do this Troy andrew Lewis?Yes sir that's me .I am officer   Carl tozer with the united states marshals office.What can i do for you sir? Asks Troy.W ell it may be more appropriate for us to ask you what we can do for you.

Sir I have to get these cows milked. Would it be ok if I continued to milk them while you talk to me? Sure thats fine.Mr Lewis in the middle of the night on sept 2nd 2000 at ruffly sometime between 130am and 415 am 2 people were shot at the north bound haverhill massachusetts rest area off of interstate i 495.One man was shot to death mr .Lewis the other sustained a bullet through his shoulder and collar bone that night but he lived.Now unbeknownst to you you sir these people were part of the 3rd largest drug chain up and down the east coast of the united states.I know you were the drop man cause i can tell.

I sat in an unmarked car at the mcdonalds restaurant across the street And took many photo and camera shots of you.I also know the plate number of our toyota out of maine.47a-8at me correct? Yes sir I can also tell you that that car was towed from your cousins house in lincoln maine to our federal impound yard in portland maine.Sir can i ask you a question? Sure Replied marshall tozer.Can i atleast finish milking these cows before you arrest me?I'm not here to arrest you.Then what is the urgency of talking to me at the crack of dawn? Like i said young man unbeknownst to you, you stumbled into the 3rd biggest drug ring on the eastern seaboard.Yes but i transported drugs across the international border and i hauled drugs known for the purpose of trafficking.All federal offences that carry arrest judge jury and improsoment if found guilty correct?Correct to the letter mr Lewis did you once have a attorney background? No sir but you probably already know everything about me so you know i've had a scrape or 2 with the law in my 38 yrs of life.So i don't understand why aren't you gonna arrest me.Mr Lewis do you have any idea how much money the Halifax to boston drug traffic business is worth a year?

Id say around 5.3 to 5.5 million.Thats about right do have any idea how much the 3rd biggest one produces?11 12 million a year? Try 40 million a year? Wow replied Troy.so what do you want from me marshall tozer.it's simple the gun that shot those 2 men that night was never found never discovered.

All we know is it was a glock by the bullets we dug out of them.whats that gun have to do with me replied Troy?Both men shot that nite were members of the abiluabilqua cartel.So what does that have to do with me replied Troy .Cause if i can get that gun fingerprint it and find who killed these 2 guys my operation is not compromised.But i don't understand was the Halifax syndicate involved?Why was you watching me? Compared to the the 3rd biggest drug ring were small potatoes.Yes but we didn't know who the 3rd

Biggest players were involved with. So you suspected Halifax syndicate could have a connection .But that's what we didn't know.thats why that night you were allowed to make your drop collect the cash get in your car and leave.But your still not answering my question sir.How does 2 people getting shot at a rest area in haverhill massachusetts in the middle of the night and the gun not found compromise your operation?Mr Lewis do you have any idea

who the united states of america's oldest and most law respected office is? I'm not sure replies Troy, Maybe the fbi, in Canada i know its the rcmp.

Mr Lewis in america its the us marshals office.those 2 men shot that nite were members of the abiluabilqua cartel,they were both hispanic american citizens one born in miami, the other born in baltimore maryland.And both veteran federal bureau investigation officers.F.B.I!!!!!!!!!!???? Your telling me the 3rd biggest drug business on the eastern seaboard of this great nation is run and fronted by the f b i it seems to appear so.So you see officer samuel mateo garcia he won't be talking he's 0 liability He is in the ground pushing up daisies.That was the man's name that was shot to death?Yes a 14 yr veteran of the fbi. But fbi officer Ricky alejandro perez is alive and well at a federal

Correction prison in louisville kentucky. He is being held for an assault charge on his wife, and screaming louder and louder everyday mr Lewis.H e was sentenced to 3 yrs for assault and battery to his wife .But he served 3 yrs and 9 days as a model prisoner.His paperwork has gotten shuffled and lost so thats why hes not released as of yet but i can't legally hold him much longer.And he's threatening to go to every newspaper, radio, tv station he can

Find and sing like a canary about the bad things the fbi does The gun is crucial, if i can find that gun and get a print and bring in whoever shot these 2 pieces of trash .Well i may be able to put him away for good.So what are you saying officer tozer ? the gun is linked to me? No i'm not saying that but i've turned over every possible stone to this investigation 4 or 5 times trying to get something and all I've got is one dead thug and another one in jail about to soon be released and to hurt and embarrass our nation.

Mr. Lewis, I took an oath at 18 years of age to protect and defend and serve this country and our constitution when I signed up for the United States Marines .

At 24 years of age i took an oath to protect and defend and serve this great nation of ours when i was 24 years of age when i became a US marshall mr Lewis that was 19 years ago for my US marshall oath and 25 years ago for my united states marine oath.Have you ever made an oath to anything mr Lewis? Yes sir , I've made an oath to follow the lord Jesus Christ for the rest of my days.W ell that's a very noble oath mr Lewis.So im sure you understand how crucial oaths are.officer Tozer give me a few days to think on this.You know if we have your full cooperation in this we could wipe your record clean.A nd if i don't cooperate sir?

Last guy i heard that was linked to the the abiluabilqua interruption of daily drug flow was found with his hands tied to his ankle bones and a drill bit handle in his right eyes socket and a ⅞" 15 inch long drill bit drilled clear out to the back of his skull.Not pretty.Here's my card mr . Lewis, I hope you're in touch with me in the next few days.officer tozer walked out of the barn and about 5 seconds later Troy threw up between the water troff and the feed bin.

Maybe it was the thought of the drill bit from one end of the guy's skull to the other , maybe it was the thought of this nightmare never being over.But whatever it was it caused Troy sickness and worry.

Troy grabbed the water bottle and rinsed out his mouth.he got the milking done and looked at his watch. 718 am pastor tom should be up by now he goes into the house and is greeted by randy. Good morning Troy i slept in a little this morning.I am on my way to the store i just made a fresh pot of coffee help yourself. Shirley is just up in the shower have a great day. I'm on my way to the store. Bye bye.
Bye Randy, have a nice day. You to young man.Troy looks on the wall at the list of numbers.Pastor tom house phone.He dials the number three rings no answer 4 rings he hears a familiar voice hello.Hi pastor tom it's Troy, Troy Lewis.Hi Troy how are you.Im ok listen Pastor tom a situation has crept into my life uninvited and very quickly.And i need some advice and guidance on how to handle it could u talk to me asap? Sure Troy id be happy to. well can you today? Yes, what time works good for you? Well i do my evening milking at 6pm i will be done that at 830 pm would nine work out ok pastor tom?Yes 9 would be excellent the sunday school dept has Christmas practice for the pageant tonight from 630 pm to 830 so 9 pm would work out lovely!!! Ok ill meet you at your office door at 9 pm ok Troy .Oh and pastor i want to take lacey if she will come .Does it involve her? No not directly but i

admire her counsel and wisdom to .Then by all means bring her Troy.Ok thank you see you tonight.Troy looks back at the list of numbers and phones olivers country store.one ring no answer .2 rings he hears a sweet soothing calming voice.Olivers country store. Lacey it's Troy.Well hey sugar plum what a nice surprise this is.How are you? Im ok listen can you do me a huge favour? Sure sugar plum shoot.well i am having a meeting with pastor tom tonight ,and i'd like you to come with me if you're able. You know i will

What time is it at? Ohh lacey thank you thank you a million times thank u. Your welcome.its at 9pm

Could u pick me up at home at 840 pm?sure no problem sugar plum. Thank you lacey have a great day at work dear , you to sugar plum

I really really appreciate this lacey. I value and treasure your opinion deeply. Thanks for going with me.Bye bye lacey.

As Troy went through his day it seemed to take forever to reach 840pm

But it came and like clockwork Lacey was there to pick him up.

On the way over to the church he told lacey it was about his past

Lacey was very kind calm and reassuring to Troy sugar plum dont worry

God has this for you.

As lacey and Troy went into pastor toms office to talk to talk about everything Troy laid it all out to pastor tom every detail he expected lacey to run out of the room and tell him it's over but lacey just sat there quietly and intensively listing to every detail listing to every word. After Troy spoke his last word, Lacey and pastor tom sat there in silence then after about 20 seconds pastor tom asked lacey and Troy to hold his hands as they prayed.

Pastor Tom begins to pray dear Jesus please guide my lips and my mind on directing Troy in your counsel lord.A nd lord please send him a reassurance and peace that your ways are the best ways.In Jesus name we ask this in Jesus name amen.

So Troy one of the 2 men you shot died that is correct?

Yes pastor tom sadly thats true.

Yes pastor tom and also the massachusetts authorities have no inkling your involved in any way.That's correct sir.There were no cameras in the massachusetts rest areas prior to that happening but now every single one in the

State has one.You have been carrying this secret a long time.Yes pastor

I want to do what's right.But im afraid if i do whats right its just a matter of time before the abiluabilqua cartel hunts me down and puts a bullet in my head.Maybe replies pastor tom maybe not that attack on you may have been just them.Being greedy for the money. Maybe nobody knew.

Pastor may i say something asks lacey oh yes lacey by all means replies pastor tom.Troy deep down within you no matter what happens to you

You know and understand and realise that you're a child of the most high king don't you?Yes lacey i understand this.Nobody is gonna do anything to you unless god wills it.The marshalls name that talked to me was officer carl tozer. He said they could help me in any way he could. you feel about this Troy,asks pastor tom? I've repented many many times to god about the night that i shot the 2 men that jumped me and tried to rob me of that drug money.And i believe god has forgiven me. I am very ashamed of the Troy Lewis i used to be. But i'm not ashamed of the Troy Lewis i am and becoming.

And pastor i have asked lacey to be my girlfriend, and i'm so happy and glad she said yes.In the future i want all of this behind me and be able to go down the street with my head held high as a testimony of god and his goodness to me.Well Troy that's very very admirable says pastor tom.Lacey how do you feel about all this?asks pastor tom .Pastor god never ever once has given up on me, so i don't want to give up on Troy.

Well Troy to me it sounds cut and dried replied pastor tom i would contact officer tozer tell him the whereabouts of the gun and admit to what you done then immediately after you do all this i would ask him what the U s marshalls office is prepared to do for your well being.Lacey do you have anything to add? No pastor i take the position that Troy takes id want done and over with as quick as possible but Troy

Know that God and i are here with you and we will remain to be with you.Thank you lacey replies Troy as he smiles.And Troy know that i and the church are here for you as well.Thanks well it's settled ill call officer tozer at 9 am sharp tomorrow morning.they close in a word of prayer.Troy asks lacey to drive him to sonic drive in Troy treats lacey and himself to a strawberry milkshake and that just talk and hold hands until the clock strikes midnight.

Then lacey takes him home as Troy exits the vehicle she says to Troy

Remember sugar plum ,Gods got this in his hands don't you fret and worry .Thank you lacey replied Troy.I'll stop by after work tomorrow and you can tell me what officer tozer tells you ok? Ok says Troy.Night lacey good night sugar plum.Troy goes into the house, pours a big glass of milk,Goes into his bedroom and begins to pray. Lord im gonna call officer tozer and do what's right please be with me and help me.And with that prayer Troy climbs into bed and falls fast asleep.After the morning milking some eggs gathered Troy enjoys

A hearty breakfast with randy and shirley 858 am almost time.Troy can shirley and i pray with you.I would love that replies Troy.Father as this young man makes this call please be with him give him the words to say allow mercy and divine providence to be with this young man as he is trying to do whats right.We ask all this in Jesus name.Amen.

Thank you shirley and randy your welcome.Thay smile and reply. Troy takes the business card out of his pocket and dials officer tozers number.

1 ring no answer, 2 rings no answer 3 rings.Us marshall tozer speaking .Marshall carl tozer? Yes . Officer this is Troy Lewis. Good morning Troy how are you? Asks officer T ozer.Im ok thank you and yourself ?

Just fine, thank you. Officer tozer do you have a pen and paper because i have a lot to say and you may wanna write it down.Well to start with i don't know how much or to what extent you will help me .But i know alot about that night those 2 men were shot in massachusetts.Ok go on i'm listening.Well to start officer your right it was a glock that shot those 2 men.And i know who owned the gun I know where the gun came from i can tell you the year and season but i'm unsure of the specific date .I know where the gun is now,and i know who shot those men? Can you prove who shot them Troy.I can't prove it for the fingerprints were wiped from the gun. Ok do you know his name?Yes i do but before i tell you the person who shot them, shot them in self defense.You were there to witness the man do that Troy? No sir officer tozer.But i know the man who shot them got jumped in the washroom they attempted to rob him.You were told this by someone Troy? No sir, I am the man that jumped, I am the man who shot them and I am the man who knows the whereabouts of that gun. As Troy shares all the details with marshall tozer he ends by saying this.Yes sir contact st stephen new brunswick Canada office for royal canadian mounted police tell they will find the gun buried ruffly 5 to 7 inches in the ground between 88 and 90 civic address on old bay road but closer to 90 .Its ruffly 30 ft off the road there was a clump of white birch trees and a big pine tree i buried it ruffly 4 ft behind that pine tree.

Troy thank you very much for this information.Your welcome marshall tozer.But what do i do now?What do you mean ask's marshall tozer ? Well will there be an active warrant for my arrest? Am i going to face murder 1 charges and assult with a weapons charge whats going on? Troy i can promise you these two things if anyone is going to arrest you it will be me personally to arrest you.And i can also tell you ever member of law enforcement that i deal with will be told you are cooperating 100% in this investigation.And that you told the truth.So what should i do now officer tozer?Don't you have a farm to tend to? Yes sir Troy replies.Then pitter patter get at er ! i'll be in touch. OK .Replied Troy.Goodbye officer tozer.Goodbye Troy.Troy hangs up the phone and begins to cry profusely randy rushes to him and pulls Troy to himself shirley wraps her arms around randy and Troy and they hold Troy as he cries and cries after about one minute shirley starts to sing in a low gentle voice.What a friend we have in Jesus all our griefs and sins to bare.We should never be discouraged take it to the lord in prayer. Then randy joins in singing soft and low what a friend we have in Jesus all our sins and grief to bare. We should never be discouraged take it to the lord in prayerThey sing again and again and hold Troy tight as he cries. OH sin.Sin

sin sin. It will cost you more than you wanna pay and leave you in a twisted mess. The devil met his match today though cause if there were ever 2 angels in this world they were holding Troy while he cried. Randy and Shirley .After Troy stops crying he hugs randy, randy hugs him back then gently pushes Troy back and begins to wipe away his tears. Thank you randy. We love you Troy but most importantly God loves you!!! I know Troy smiles and says. Shirley is standing there with her arms stretched out. Troy falls into her and begins to cry again. And shirley says to him do you know what Troy? The day is gonna come when crying will cease to exist and Jesus himself will wipe all tears from your eyes.

Really it is? Ask Troy. Yes it sure is .In the book of revelation chapter 21 vs 4And god shall wipe away all tears from their eyes, and there shall be no more death nor sorrow , nor crying nor shall there be any more pain, for the former things are passed away.

So dont cry dear. One day our tears will end replies Troy.

Yes dear they will .Thank you shirley.I feel better. After Troy regains his composer he says randy could use the phone to call Canada real quick?

You sure can young man.. Thank you as Troy dials the number a soothing voice for a while makes him happy. Hello mom how are you? This is Troy. Mom imm just calling to tell you i love you!!!

Frederick Demerchant

Chapter 6 The waiting game begins

On a beautiful sunrise at 721 am randy comes into the barn.Ha ha ha ha good morning Troy, i must be getting old i just woke up 10 minutes ago.

Oh don't worry about it randy,Troy smiles and says.I got the milking all done the eggs gathered and now i was just gonna grab the chainsaw and get those bushes trimmed back away from the fence like you asked me to do.

Well lets go tackle that then go in and get a good breakfast sounds great ,Troy smiles and says.For the next hour Troy and randy are working like little beavers cutting all the bushes growing up along the fence.As the get the last of them cut ,Troy grabs themes and starts to drag them down to the tree line.when he walks back randy is leaning against a fence post, looks at Troy and smiles and says,well young man this is a lot better. Yes replies Troy bushes and weeds seem to sprout up very quickly sometimes wouldn't you agree asks Troy?For sure replies randy.You know randy that reminds me of

sin and poor choices.How do you mean?asks
randy.Well take me for instance

     When i first started running drugs i never crossed
the border with 3 duffle bags full of cocaine.Id run 15
lines, $1600 dollars worth from Halifax up to turo on a
saturday afternoon and make a quick $75 for the
weekend.It was only 55 mins up the road..But it got to
be longer and longer trips and more and more drugs
and bigger and bigger paydays for me.But then things
got so outta control ,well the next thing you know one
guy is dead,another guy is hurt badly and my future at
the best is uncertain.Randy smiles i see what your
saying ,But your long term future is set its just your short
term future that is messed up.But don't ever forget
young man the scripture that says with god all things
are possible.your his child,your eternal destiny of
heaven is sealed.Don't forget that!!Troy smiles when i
get to heaven i just wanna fall at Jesus feet and worship
him.And thank him for the cross his grace and his love
and thank him for what he's done for me.And done for
all of us!! I Believe you will get your chance one day,
Randy smiles and says. Now let's go in and have a nice
breakfast. Sounds great replied Troy.As randy and Troy
enter the house

     Troy and randy are greeted with a smile by shirley
good morning guys.

     Good morning they both smile and say the men
wash up and shirley

     Gives them 2 hot coffees and 2 saucers with
buttered toast on them for each.she grabs a box of

cheerios and a box of captain crunch and sets it on the table well i gotta go to the old folks home my shift starts in 20 minutes have a wonderful day guys!! Thanks you to they smile and say.Oh and randy says shirley.Yes dear?randy smiles and replies your gonna talk to Troy what we talked about this morning right? I sure am randy smiles and says.Have a great day dear. You as well.dear

As shirley makes her way out the door Troy pours a bowl of cheerios ,while randy has a bowl of captain crunch.Troyn asks randy ready for me to say grace to randy?I sure am randy smiles and says.Dear Jesus thank you for this food, and thank you for this day bless this food to our body's use we ask in Jesus name amen.Troy counting today, how many days has it been since you talked to marshall tozer? Umm I think it makes 10 days today replies Troy .

Still no word huh? No nothing not a peep yet.Hmm well what shirley and i talked about was we want you to know, no matter what you face and may have to endure ,we want you to know your job is here waiting for you if your away for a bit.Wow replies Troy thanks so much.Your very very welcome says randy.Were very happy with your work ,now of course if its for a little while you know a few months or something, we will have to hire someone to replace you till you get back.But when you are back the job is here for you.Thanks randy i appreciate that from the bottom of my heart.All of a sudden the phone begins to ring randy is there as the 2nd ring starts.Hello .says randy.HI randy how are you?Oh lacey dear im just fine is everything alright at the store?Oh good good.Yes hes right here dear ill get him for you ill be in ,in about 1 hour to help you ok dear?Ok you have a great morning replies randy.Troy its for

you.Thanks randy.Hello.Hi Troy how is your morning so far? Ohh its great thanks how is your morning going good?Real good Troy real good i Just wanted to tell u That im thinking about you and i hope the lord smiles down on you today! Thanks lacey how very very nice of you Troy smiles and says!!! You have a good day to Sweetheart.I will Troy bye.Bye lacey.How can life get any better?Cheerios and lacey replies randy.Shes a special girl randy .Amen to that says randy.Well i'm gonna go clean up a couple stalls you have a good day randy.You to Troy ,and remember son god loves you and shirley and i do to,thanks i won't forget and i love you and god and shirley as well.As Troy goes out and cleans the stalls in no time flat it's time for 4pm milking 2 more days roll by and still no word from officer tozer.

And like it does sunday rolls around randy shirley and Troy make there way to church and like clock work ,they pull in its 1015 am and shirley and randy are greeted by lacey in the parking lot.Good morning randy good morning shirley good morning lacey thay smile and say.Good morning sugar plum lacey smiles and says.Good morning lacey how are you? Troy smiles and says. i'm alright but i'm even better now that your here.Lacey smiles and says.They go into the house of the lord and enjoy the wonderful sermon.And music .The sermon was titled "keep climbing the mountain ,even when its hard".Troy thoroughly enjoyed that sermon.But little did he know he was going to have to put it into practice very very soon in his life.They all shake pastors toms hand and says hello.Out of a black lincoln steps out marshall carl tozer in plain clothes.Lacey and Troy are just talking with rhonda jones and mr and mrs donald and harriet gostone ,owners of the anderson roadside diner.Marshall tozer is about 6 ft from Troy and says excuse me mr Lewis?Yes Troy replied then he recognizes its marshall tozer.Oh hi Troy says.May i speak to you over in the corner of the church parking lot?Sure Troy says.When they get over there officer says ,Troy i Have some very very bad news.What is it? Troy asks

The massachusetts district attorneys office Is gonna charge you with first degree murder and assult with a weapon with intent to kill.But you told me you would do everything you could to help me.Im gonna Troy im gonna. They have set a date to arraign you at 915 am tomorrow morning.Your fLying out of spartanburg to boston logan at 4 pm this afternoon.I dressed in plain clothes where as to save you embarrassment.I appreciate that replies Troy.Your welcome listen you go say goodbye to your friends than get my car.Don't say anything to me until you get to the anderson police station.I'll read your rights ,and place you under arrest there. I need you to know im gonna do everything i can to help you. I'll put the handcuffs on you just before we go into the police station ok.Thank you officer tozer.As Troy walks over to lacey he beckons for shirley and randy to come over to him.He informs shirley and randy and Lacey what is going on they hold hands and pray .And then each one hugs him.Lacey and Troy walk over to officer tozers car.Lacey gives him one more hug and whispers in his ear.Dont worry or be afraid.God is with you remember what Jesus said in hebrews 13 ;5 i will never leave thee nor forsake thee.You remember that ok. And know i love you and i'm praying for you!!! I Love you to lacey.Replied Troy.Troy gets into officer tozers car.As he drives out Troy looks behind him and thinks to himself,I love this church.I Love these people i sure hope i see them soon.Then he silently prays unto himself:Lord i told you i'm gonna serve you for the rest of my days and i meant it.But right now is where the rubber hits the road i don't know what im gonna face.But please help me and give me favor.I ask all this in Jesus name.Amen

After a few mins they arrive at the anderson police station.They ring the button and a mans voice comes across the intercom.Anderson police station how may i help you? This is united states marshall carl tozer I have a suspect in custody wanted in the state of massachusetts on charges.Ok hold on i'll buzz you in.As the buzzer rings to open the door,Troy and marshall tozer enter the building .They walk down a long hallway and and the voice that greeted them on the intercom says good morning marshall tozer .Good morning replies officer tozer.May i see your badge and id please officer ?Yes sir he removes it from his flannel shirt pocket and shows it to the young officer.The officer looks at it and hands it back to officer tozer.Thank you us marshall tozer,im officer brian stevens with the anderson police service. Hi officer stevens i would like a room to take this suspect into please and remove these handcuffs off his wrist.Yes sir.I will be done interviewing this suspect in about 7 minutes he leaves soon for spartanburg airport is there a comfortable cell he could rest in? And perhaps a food and drink he could be given.

Yes sir replies officer stevens.After marshall tozer read Troy his Miranda rights and placed him under arrest he says : would you like a lawyer appointed to you now Troy? No replied Troy.I will take a lawyer up in massachusetts.Ok replied officer tozer.As marshall tozer tells officer stevens they were ready for that cell.Officer stevens gently takes Troys right forearm and escorts him into his holding cell.He closes the door and looks inside and says ill be right back.In about 3 minutes the officer returns with a ham and swiss sandwich on rye an apple and a bottle of orange juice.Thank you so much Troy looks at the young policeman and replies.Your welcome.As officer stevens sits down ,officer tozer walks up to him and says.Officer stevens i have to go get another marshall who is gonna escort and guard mr.Lewis .Ok replied officer stevens.Please see that he's comfortable sir.I will.

As Troy bowed his head and gave thanks for his food he noticed the officer had a local Christain radio station on.Excuse me?Troy said to the young police officer.Yes sir replied,.Officer stevens .Do you know Christ he asks as he finishes eating.Yes sir replied officer stevens.for almost 7 years now.Thats great replied Troy.Hay we have a little bit of chocolate cake in the fridge,would u like a piece.Id never say no to chocolate cake Troy smiles and says.Thanks to you for all your kindness to me.Your welcome replied the young policeman.Troy finishes the cake and sets the dishes on top of the little shelf in the cell.He lays down on the bed but only for 13 or 14 mins then officer tozer shows back up.Troy sticks his hands behind his back and backs up against the door officer tozer buts the handcuffs on him.They open the door and escort him out to the car.officer tozer says to the young policeman ,thanks for all your help and assistance.Your welcome us marshall tozer.

marshall tozer and Troy and the other young Us marshall, drive over to spartanburg.marshall tozer has the am radio tuned to a news channel ,Troy sits in back just looking around at the countryside. Troy thinks to himself i sure hope i'm back here very very soon, but i don't know, but i hope.But then he thinks to himself i am alive ,Ihave the love of shirley, lacey and randy in my life.I just have this last bit of trouble to clear out of my life,then by god and his dear sweet grace all this trouble and strife will be behind me.As they arrive at the spartanburg airport officer tozer says to Troy.Mr Lewis this is us marshall   phillip danse.He has been with the marshalls service going on 4 years now.He is a good man Troy.He as been briefed by me in full and he has committed to me he's gonna do his absolute best to help in any way he can to.

Thank you marshalls tozer and danse , i so appreciate all your folks goodness and kindness to me.Marshall tozer replies psalm 146;7 which executeth judgement for the oppressed: witch giveth food to the hungry. The lord looseth the prisoners. Mr. Lewis, remember how you told me you made that commitment and oath to follow Christ? Yes sir replied Troy.Do your best to honour that and watch and see what the lord will do. Marshall danse will be with you right up till arraignment tomorrow morning.I Have a few loose ends i will be tying up here tomorrow morning.By lunch time tomorrow ,i will be on my way to boston to help you because in my experience they like to move fast on these things.Ok thank you marshall tozer.As marshall danse opens the back door and and escorts Troy out.In no time flat they are seated and taxiing down the runway.The stewardess gave marshall danse and Troy a bag of peanuts and an ice cold coca cola apiece while they are inflight. And in no time flat They are landing in boston logan.As marshall danse is escorting Troy off the plane ,the reality of everything that is taking place is really hitting home to Troy.But Troy knows and trusts that gods gonna help him with everything.

As Troy walks up the gangway into the main part of the airport shackled in handcuffs ,he is met by 3 state troopers of massachusetts.Us marshall danse? One of them says to marshall danse im officer joe eaglewood with the massachusetts state troopers.I Have a squad car around front for mr Lewis.ok marshall danse replies.I will help you escort him to your squad car. Ok replies officer eaglewood.So with one state trooper walking in front of him,one behind him Us marshall danse to his right and trooper eaglewood to his left,They make their way to the squad car through the airport.It's snowing quite hard as they open the door and put Troy into the back of the car.Us marshall his arraignment is tomorrow morning i understand you are going to be at that arraignment?Yes sir replied us marshall danse.Ok we're gonna take him to the courthouse holding jail for tonight.Ok sir i trust you officers can take it from here? Yes sir .Replies officer eaglewood.Ok i have a rental car booked through hertz rent a car i have to go in and pick up then drive over to my motel.Plus i have to go to baggage claim and pick up my suitcase.Ok well we shall see you in the morning marshall danse.OK as Troy is taken away to the courthouse holding jail.us marshall danse gets his car and luggage and drives over to the ramada inn.

As Troy is put into his cell and the door gently shut behind him.Officer eaglewood says to Troy.I am going to get u a cppl boxes of small cereal thats all we have in this facility your choices are special k .frosted flakes or post grape nuts.Troy replies ill have grape nuts please.i am gonna return with a little carton of milk and a bottle of water for you to drink inside your cell there

Is a towel ,sink , flush bed blanket and pillow and a bar of soap. At 530 am you will be awakened and given something to eat.Then at 6 am ,you will be given a list of lawyers names and phone numbers u can choose one to represent you and call him.Would you like your 1 phone call tonight after you eat?Yes if that would be ok replies Troy.Thats ok says officer eaglewood.

I will return shorty with the food and drink and then ill come back in about 20 minutes

and let you make that phone call ok?Ok thank you says Troy.

After about 20 mins Troy disposes of his water bottle and plastic spoon and styrofoam bowl in the garbage can by the sink.then around 5 or 6 mins later officer eaglewood places him in cuffs takes him over by the phone and says just dial 1 and your area code then your number.You have 20 minutes.Thank you says Troy.on the 3rd ring a beautiful voice is on the other end of the phone .Hello .Lacey its Troy.How are you sweetheart?Sugar plum im ok how are you doing?Im good thank you lace.Did they feed you sugar plum?Oh yes a police officer in anderson gave me lunch then i had peanuts and a coca cola on the plane and i just finished my supper now.Fantastic sugar plum .I got great news for you sugar plum .Pastor tom called me we got 5 different churches from 3 different counties praying for you and your situation.Your the best lacey!! Its my honour sugar plum now don't you get discouraged ok?.I wont lacey .Do you have my mom and dad's phone number? Yes, I sure do sugar plum.

Will you please call them soon and let them know that i've made it here and im doing good.I'll call them soon as i am off the phone with you.ok sugar plum ill also call randy and shirley after that and give them an update to.Thank you lacey i appreciate all your help.No problem Can we pray together lacey? we sure can lacey says.In what seemed to be no time flat officer eaglewood walks over and says mr Lewis 2 minutes.

After the prayer Troy says ill call you as soon as i can.And please tell pastor tom i said thank you for all the prayers and please thank all the other churches for praying for me to.You welcome sugar plum.Bye lacey.Bye bye sugar plum.Troy hangs up the phone and officer eaglewood places him back into his cell

Troy gets on his knees and silently prays for 3 or 4 minutes rolls down his sheets closes his eyes and goes to sleep.

Chapter 7 : Troy goes before the judge

Mr Lewis ,Mr Lewis time to awaken, says an older gentleman jail guard.Troy turns his sheets down. What time is it he asks the guard? Its 527 am.Mr Lewis what would u like for your cereal this morning?I will have special k please.Do you want a cup of coffee?Oh that would be lovely replies Troy!!!!what do you take in it? 2 cream 2 sugar please.The guard returns with a styrofoam cup of coffee a little box of special k cereal and a plastic spoon styrofoam bowl and a small carton of milk.Thank you replies Troy your welcome.replies the guard.truy finishes his breakfast and disposes of the garbage in the garbage can in his holding cell. Goes over to his bed side to pray.Dear lord thanks so much for all you have done for me in my life.And especially the blessings of late such as randy shirley pastor tom and lacey.

God thank you for my mom and dad you have given me.Please forgive me when i was younger and had taken them for granted.Please forgive me of that!!! God i ask that you will be with me in that courtroom today.Please help me father.But no matter what happens today remember,i love you.And i am committed to serving you.Thanks for all you have done for me in Jesus name amen.Troy gets up off his knees and stands over by his cell door he looks up

At the clock 553 am .Not long now before I can look at the lawyer list and call.Mr Lewis ,calls out the guard,Yes sir . replies Troy.Turn around by the holding cell door place your hands behind your back.I have to handcuff you before i can take you down to the room you're gonna use to call your lawyer.

As Troy has his hands placed in cuffs, the guard escorts him down the hall.He takes him in and uncuffs him.He goes out and flicks on the intercom.Mr Lewis in the centre of the table you will see 2 sheets of paper.

They are all a list of law firms that will represent you .And send an attorney here within the hour to go over your case through the small window Troy mouths thank you to the guard. Your welcome Mr Lewis just pick up the phone and dial the number.Troy looks down the list.J.A. smith and son law firm specialising in criminal ,real estate and corporate law. Troy thinks to himself probably not a good fit. Harrison, Fitch and Sanderson .Specialising in tax law. Headley g donaldson attorney at law. Doesn't feel anything there.

Devine law practice.He stops looks back over it again.The word divine

Almost seems to be illuminated.He rubs his eyes looks again

Sure enough the word devine almost seems to be lit up.Troy looks up

To the ceiling.Lord you don't have to tell me twice!! He smiles and says!!! He dials the number and a voice answers on the other end:Devine law practice,How may i help you.

Yes good morning my name is Troy Lewis .I am remanded in custody at the boston court house,227 haston street.Ok says the receptionist voice.What are you remanded into custody for?I have been charged with 1st degree murder.And a 2nd charge of assult with a deadly weapon with intent to kill.

And how are you going to be pleading today sir? Not guilty.Alright the current time is 609 am we will have a lawyer there by 715 am to go over your case and represent you.Ok that's great ,thank you so much.Your welcome,Is there anything else i can do for you?No that's it, replied Troy.But thank you so much.Your welcome Mr Lewis goodbye.Goodbye.Troy notices a button on the wall that says, push to talk on intercom.,

Troy says to the guard, my phone call is complete a lawyer is gonna be here by 715 am to go over my case and represent me.Ok replied the guard. W ould you like to wait in this room, or be escorted back to your cell?I can wait here, but i was wondering may you folks have

a little tube of toothpaste a toothbrush a disposable razor and a small can of shaving cream .So as to brush my teeth and shave?The guard replies no i'm sorry,we are just an overnight holding facility we don't have anything like that here.. Its ok nreplied Troy.Do you need to use the restroom or anything?No im good but thank you.Would u like another cup of coffee or a bottle of water? A bottle of water would be great says Troy thank you very much.You are most welcome ill go get that for you. The Guard grabs it and drops it in the slot hole of the door for Troy.Troy pushes the button.Thank you.Troy looks up at the wall.7;13 am in 2 hrs and 2 mins ill be before the judge.The reality of everything is really sinking in now.And just like clock work at 715 am sharp the guard opens the door and a very very fat man,short and fat he's probably 5ft 5 inches and weighs about 239 lbs walks in.Im mr ralph lunsden with divine law practice.Good morning sir.replied Troy.Ralph sticks out his hand and shakes it.Mr Lewis , our receptionist helen told me your facing 2 charges today? Yes sir im facing murder one and asult with a deadly weapon with intent to kill.Ok and she told me you wish to plead innocent of these charges.Yes sir.Mr Lewis you were accosted and attacked in a bathroom in a rest area in haverhill massachusetts correct? Yes sir. There were no cameras in those places so all i can do is
Hope that they will believe me it was in self defense.Yes mr Lewis after this event happened ,the state of massachusetts installed cameras in all rest

Areas statewide. That's a good thing at least that has happened from this horrible event.

Mr Lewis i read on your police report ,that the united states marshals office is involved with this case?Yes sir i had a Us marshall visit me at the place of my work.And where would that be sir? Asks mr lunsden.My place of work is hilltop farm in anderson south carolina.Mr lunsden opens up his briefcase and removes a hilroy scribbler and a pen.Ok and now when this Us marshall visited you what did he inform you of?He informed me that i had been under surveillance for what i was doing?So you did not know that you were delivering drugs to the 3rd biggest drug operation on the east coast? No sir that is correct.I thought that i was bringing drugs to my usual customer.And who would that usual customer be mr Lewis?It would be the Halifax to boston cocaine syndicate sir.officer tozer"thats the us marshall who visited me" was
Letting me go he told me to not compromise his investigation.

Ok replied mr lunsden but why is the Us marshalls office trying to help with this case in a charge of you for murder, and assult
 with a deadly weapon with intent to kill? Because mr lunsden the 2 men that attacked me are directly involved with the 3rd biggest drug operation on americas east coast. And in more ways than one.What do you mean in more ways then one?asks mr lunsden.Sir these 2 men are active ,well one still as

active member of the abiluabilqua cartel.Ok .replied mr .lunsden that doesn't surprise me anything bad to do with drugs from chicago east usually involves them in one way or another.ok so where they are active abiluabilqua cartel members that's definitely one way they are involved.What is the other way thay are directly involved?asks mr lunsden.Samuel mateo garcia and Ricky alejandro perez were both veteran f.b.i.officers? WHAT!!!!?? Replied mr lunsden. Troy you're telling me that both men that attacked you and tried to rob you in haverhill massachusetts are and were Fbi agents.Thats what

was told to me by Us marshall officer tozer mr.lunsden.And it gets worse?

Mr Lunsden scratches his head how could it possible get worse?asks mr.lunsdem.Mr tozer believes all the Fbi is involved in this.Mr lunsden gets up out of this chair .He puts his hands on his hips and walks around and says this is bad this is really really bad!!!mr lunsden,mr lunsden? Mr lunsden just keeps walking around with his hands on his hips.This is bad this is bad.He quickly walks over to Troy and sticks his face about 2 inches from Troys face and says mr Lewis do you realize the massive corruption thats going on here if this is true!!? Well I'm no lawyer but that's why I believe the Us marshals office is fighting for me.

I would think the best thing you could do is call a meeting with

Officer tozer, mr lunsden.Oh by the sounds of all this
there will be quite a few meetings!!!   Sir i'm not an
attorney but everything I'm telling you is true.Mr lunsden
walks back over to his chair and sits down.Man talk
about a wild way to start my work week!! Replies mr
lunsden.I just hope you and officer tozer
Can get to the bottom of what's happening and my
name will be cleared.

Mr lunsden removes the handkerchief from his pocket
and wipes his forehead and neck.Young man one thing i
am concerned with is your safety. From the
Abiluabilqua cartel or someone else? Well to be honest
with you young man
In my 27 yrs of law practice,most of this stuff is like.is
like.well.Its like an onion the more layers you peel the
more it stinks.Well sir i don't know what your personal
beliefs are, but i'm a Christian. I walked away from god
once, but im
not gonna again.So i believe what will be will be .But i
want to get this done, and get it behind me.Iam very
very sorry one of those men died and the other one got
hurt very badly, but i am not a murder it was self
defense.Well i admire your faith young man.Replied Mr
lunsden but lets just enter the plea and we will go from
there.Mr lunsden? Yes young man i believe you're the
right man for the job, i believe god sent you to me. I
hope so young man, i hope so. I hope so.Well what do
you think and recommend now mr.lumsden?
Mr. lumsden looks up at the clock on the wall its 653
am. We have 1 hour and 37 mins we can go over

everything.At 830 am 2 court officers are gonna come and do a pat down search on you then escort you up to the courtroom, where you will enter your plea with the judge.Then once your taken into that room,They will search me then i will be allowed to rejoin you.We can go over any last minute things about your case.After this the judge will read the charges brought up against you.And either you or i can enter a plea of guilty or not guilty to these charges.

So I think the best thing we can do is ,go over every single detail of that nite.
Ohh and mr.Lewis remember if the judge asks you a direct question.Clear concise and to the point answers.If advise something shouldn't be said i will
Advise you to stop ok?Ok mr .Lunsden.First thing i would like to do is say a prayer for you and my situation unto God.Ok? Sure young man that would be fine.Dear God please help mr Lunsden to guide my case.Lord i believe you sent this man to me.Give him the wisdom and tools he needs to represent me
Properly and so I can face what I have to face, put it behind me .I ask all this in Jesus name amen.

While mr.lumsden and Troy go over every angle and aspect of that nite,what seems to be in no time flat the guards enter the room for a patdown search of Troy.And in no time flat mr. lumsden leaves the room and Troy is patted down.

Mr. lumsden exits the room and proceeds to go to
courtroom 2 d as instructed by the guards.At 847 am
the guards escort Troy in beside mr lumsden.Troy looks
all around at the big courtroom and the big giant desk
where the judge will preside over him.In what seems to
be no time at all Troy hears the words.
All rise the honourable judge Arnold smith presiding.you
may be seated. replies judge smith.We are here today
for docket number Ma 275322
The state of Massachusetts versus Troy Andrew Lewis.
Mr. Lewis you are charged by the state of
Massachusetts district attorneys office on 2 counts.
First degree murder of Samuel mateo garcia and assult
with a weapon with intent to kill to Ricky alejandro
perez.How do you plead mr Lewis? Not guilty, your
honour.

Your honour may I address the bench? I am mr. Ralph
lunsden,Mr Lewis's attorney.Yes you may replies judge
smith.
Your honour we request the presence of the Us
marshals service when this
goes to trial.Objection your honour shouts out attorney
Christopher flynn, representing the state of
massachusetts .The state has charged Mr. Lewis with
these crimes it has nothing to do with the Us marshals
service.Your honour may i address the court?asks
attorney lunsden.Yes you may replies judge smith.Your
honour the Us marshals office has direct involvement on
the nite that these terrible things happened. also mr
Lewis informed me that officer us marshall carl tozer

has informed him he has certified letters ,along with registered mail , where he has made lots of attempts for direct involvement to request to be involved.A ll of a sudden a young man stands up in court and raises his hand.Your honour may I address the court? Asks the young man.Young man please state your name and what do you wanna address the court about? Objection your honour objection shouts out attorney flynn.Your honour my name is Donald martin i'm a Us marshall with the Us marshals office of boston.Hold on young man.Replies judge smith.Court officer go back to mr martin, get his marshalls id and badge and bring it to me please.The court officer walks back to Us marshall martin and gets what judge smith requested.The court officer hands it to the judge .Judge smith looks at his badge and I.D. and asks him to return it to the young marshall.Proceed officer martin says judge smith.Every word attorney lunden has told you is true.The Us marshals office of boston has made 3 attempts to be involved if and when mr Lewis would go to trial. Twice by us postal service registered mail and once by certified letter dropped off to the court by ups parcel service.Proceed young man. Says judge smith .Also your honour from the anderson south carolina office we tried twice by ups parcel service by certified letter and once by registered letter through the us postal office.Also your honour several times through phone calls from our boston office anderson south carolina office and once from our camden new jersey office.I have a copy of the phone records on me in person if

you would like to see them your honour.Says us
marshal officer martin.No that is fine replies judge smith.
Attorney Flynn, why was the Us marshals office never
replied to?Your honour says attorney flynn.I was never
ever notified that there trying to contact our office,but as
asked before i object this its the state of massachusetts
bringing charges against mr Lewis .We would like it if
you would honour our request and not have the Us
marshals office involved.Attorney flynn your objection is
overruled .I will allow the Us marshals office to get
involved in attending this case.As america's oldest and
most reputable law office ,they are certainly welcome in
my courtroom.
Attorney lunsden, attorney flynn if i set the trial date for
915 am exactly 3 weeks

From today are you both good? We will be ready to
proceed your honour replies attorney flynn.Your honour
may i turn and ask us marshall martin a
question? Yes you may replied judge smith.Officer
marshall does this give the marshalls office enough time
to prepare where judge smith has allowed your
participation? Yes sir replied officer martin.Ok i am
setting the trial date of mr Lewis verses the state of
massachusetts for 915 am 3 weeks from today.Now the
matter of bail says judge smith. Your honour the D.A. 's
office asks for no bail to be set for mr .Lewis.On what
application attorney flynn? Your honour
We feel mister Lewis poses a great flight risk.Over ruled
on this U s marshals report it says Mr flynn was very
cooperative.Mr Lewis bail is set for you by this court for

the sum of $685000 dollars.Troy and attorney lunsden talky for a moment amongst themselves,Your honour says attorney lunsden, Mr Lewis cannot make bail today your honour.Thank you attorney lunsden.I judge Arnold Smith hereby remand Mr Troy Lewis in custody until 915 am january 8th.Or until bail can be met.All rise.Mr Lewis i hereby remand you into custody into the state penitentiary in Worcester massachusetts. The bailiff users Troy to the holding cell until prison transportation comes to get him.As Troy waits in his Cell, he prays a little prayer.God i thank you today for bringing me attorney lunsden.I thank you that the judge smith is allowing the Us marshals office to be involved.And i pray you will give the strength wisdom and grace to endure what i have to endure,to put these horrible things behind me once and for all.

As the prison van comes to pick up Troy and take him to the federal penitentiary, Troy hopes the 21 days will move quicker rather than slower.

But a state penitentiary is no place to be for years on end or 21 days.But God almighty and his grace is everywhere including state prisons.

Chapter 8 Prayers, Presents and an interesting person.

Well lacey have you heard from Troy lately dear?
No but tomorrow is Christmas eve and i'm hoping they
will let him call then or Christmas day.I know shirley and
i really miss him at the farm and at home.You know its
funny you should say that randy.The last time we talked
i said Troy, i'm so happy and glad that God sent you to
me ,Shirley and randy.God love him randy he giggled
and said lacey im sorry but you guys are wrong God
sent all you wonderful folks into my life.Aww God love
him randy smiles and says.
As this conversation is going on ,a young lady comes in
smiles and says as she looks at randy and lacey and
says ,good morning Yall where can i find
Your dish detergent at?It's on the 3rd isle half way down
randy smiles and says.Thank y'all says the young
lady.Lacey dear don't forget when u leave today out
back in your slot box there's a card and a little
Christmas bonus in it for ya.Aww thanks randy how kind

of you.It's my pleasure dear oh and before 8 pm stop by the house we got a turkey in the freezer for you to.Aww thank you i will.Please by 8pm no later shirley and i will be in bed after that.Tell ya i really miss Troy at those 4 am milkings!!! Ha ha ha randy chuckles and says.

How are you doing with those randy Asks lacey? Ohh it's good I got a student hired to help out but I'm not gonna lie we really miss Troy. Oh don't get me wrong the young student has a great work ethic but this is only his 2nd job in his life and he just dont got the work experience Troy has.A nd you know what lacey i think all his years of logging has really helped with his farm job.Interesting how so? Asks lacey.Well when he was logging he said if something broke but it was just little you would try to rig it up somehow to get through the rest of the day so you wouldn't loose production, and ultimately money.And let me tell you what, does that ever come in handy on the farm!!!

I imagine so replied lacey.Lacey dear did u check the schedule for tomorrow?

Yes I did replied lacey, im off at 1pm tomorrow? Yes dear im closing the store down at 3pm and we will open at 6 am on the 26th.I thought id let u knock off a cppl hours early and get ready for the Christmas eve service at 630 pm and do a lil last minute shopping if you have any to do!! Aww thanks randy replies lacey.Are you gonna make the Christmas eve service randy? Wouldn't miss it for the world.Randy replies.I better put a fresh pot of coffee on before the morning rush starts.I'll be over tonight around 715 pm for my turkey.And once again thank you very much to you and shirley.It's our pleasure dear god bless you and merry Christmas!!!

After the hustle and bustle of the next 2 days ,Lacey randy and shirley and rhonda are all sitting together at the Christmas eve service.After pastor tom gives a wonderful Christmas message of love and hope.And how Jesus coming into the world to give all who choose to believe love and hope.Pastor tom begins to speak to his parishioners again .Tonight as we go home to our Christmas trees and family and friends.Please let us remember those that aren't as fortunate for us. We think of those homeless tonight we think of those in poor health tonight, mentally or physically.And we think of those who would love to be with us tonight who can't be.Those who are actively deployed in military service or in prison tonight.Automatically randy, shirley, rhonda and lacey's mind all goes to Troy.They all miss him and hope he is released soon.As pastor tom prays a prayer for them they all think of Troy as they pray.
They know that god is with them in his cell,but they miss him.As the service is dismissed lacey says to randy.Randy before you go home i got a gift in my car for you and shirley.Ohh thanks lacey how very kind of you says randy.Oh your welcome says lacey if you hear from Troy tonight or tomorrow please let me know replies randy. I will reply lacey."You folks stop over tomorrow for some pecan pie" says rhonda.Well that sounds lovely says shirley we will stop over after 3pm sometime.We look forward to seeing you says randy.

Randy and Shirley goes home and turns in and waits for Christmas day.

On Christmas day thay awake and exchange gifts with each other.

The turkey smells great!! Randy says to shirley.On the other side of town lacey is just sitting down with her grandmother over a mid morning cup of tea.Grandma ,the turkey should be ready in about 1 hour.Of lovely replies rhonda that will be right around 1150 am perfect timing dear.All of a sudden the phone begins to ring .Lacey races to the phone and its Troy on the other end of the line. Hi Troy how are you doing? Hi Lacey, I'm hanging in with Jesus' help!!! That's great sugar plum merry Christmas!!! Merry Christmas to you as well lacey!!!! Thay have set my trial for 915 am january 8th ,1999.ohh im so glad replies lacey hopefully this will go to trial quickly,and you will get a very very soft sentence, and have it all behind you quickly.i hope so replies Troy but whatever the outcome, i just want to love and serve Jesus. He will be with you Troy.lacey i hope and pray this is the only Christmas we are apart. Me to sugar plum. Well i'm only allotted 7minutes for this call, can we pray very quickly?sure says lacey, ill start. Lord please be with Troy today, and every day while he awaits his trial, give him strength and grace and dont let him forget as he spends his days in prison that you love him, randy and shirley love him pastor tom and grandma and i love him. Give him peace in his heart in Jesus name amen. Dear Jesus, thanks for Lacey and her love. Thank you to Jesus for your love. I am trying to do what's right, please help me to know and to do what's right, in Jesus name amen!! Well lacey ill let you go tell your grandma i said merry Christmas . I will, replies lacey i love you sugar plum!!! And i love you lacey!!! Ill pray for you everyday!!! And i will you to lacey!!!! Bye sugar plum!!! Bye bye dear!!! Troy is e/scorted back to his cell and he lays down and goes to sleep. The last thing he remembers was looking at the lil clock radio it said 12;14 pm when he awakens its202 pm and a guard is staring into his cell

Watching him sleep.how was your sleep asks the guard, it was good replies Troy.what's your name sir ? im prison guard michael.Michael its nice to meet you i'm Troy Troy Lewis. It's a pleasure to meet you Troy!!!what is your last name, prison guard michael? Micheal smiles and says i'm just michael, well prison guard michael and Troy have some interesting laughs and conversations right up till the day of Troy's trial.at 6 am that morning, the morning of january 8th , a guard is asking Troy if he wants cereal and a banana and milk for his breakfast or coffee pancakes and oatmeal.Troy picks cereal a banana and milk.as his food tray is delivered to him Troy says excuse me ,but where is michael?who is Michael? asks the other prison guard?Michael, the prison guard who has been dealing with me and talking to me for almost 3 weeks?young man are you feeling ok? I feel fine sir why do u ask? We don't have a prison guard here named michael , i've been a guard here for over 8 years and i don't recall a michel.really says Troy? No we had a merle but i don't ever recall a michael. Huh?Troy replied. The guard bends over and picks up a

103

king james version bible that's on the floor.he picks it up and it is open to the book of chapter 13.is this yours?asks the guard? No but i would like to have it if i can. Sure not a problem says the guard.Troy takes it and begins to read hebrews chapter 13 vs 1 let brotherly love continue. Vs 2be not forgetful to entertain strangers;for thereby some have entertained angels unawares.

  As Troy lays in his cell he reads what he has in Christ in the book of ephesians.. Ephesians chapter 1 vs 7 and 8
In whom we have redemption, through his blood,the forgiveness of sins,according to the riches of his grace. Wherein he hath abounded toward us in all wisdom and prudence.
Troy read more great verses which brought him great hope and comfort for
Him to face this very very important day!!
Ephesians chapter 2 vs 10 for we are his workmanship,created in Christ Jesus unto good works,which god hath before ordained that we should walk in them.
Many things are flooding through Troy's mind as he reads the words in ephesians, but he knows that whatever the outcome of his trial, the Lord Jesus Christ has been and will be with him!!!!
As Troy's name is called by the prison guard : mr. Troy Lewis? Yes sir replies Troy, you will be leaving in 15

mins to be transported to the courthouse for your trial.ok thank you replies Troy.

Troy immediately gets off his bed, kneels on the floor and prays.Dear Lord Jesus. Your word tells us that god moves in mysterious ways.i don't know if michael was an angel i entertained unaware, but it sure does appear so. Jesus you know today i am trying to do what is right and you also know that i love you and have wholeheartedly committed my life to you.please be with me today and whatever the outcome of this trial please allow me to accept and deal with whatever comes down the line, to me and for me.i ask this all in the mighty name of Jesus.amen. As Troy is placed in handcuffs and leg shackles and escorted to the car a peace comes over him. He thinks to himself right now i am bound by shackles on my hands and feet, but I am free in Christ.

And he also thinks as i am facing a trail upon the earth today for the wrong i have done. But with god's help this will be behind me soon and i will walk the earth with no shackles physically or spiritually.

As Troy is riding to the courthouse in the back of the police car to his trial, his mind goes back to those beautiful sunday night song services and to one song in particular that him and his grandmother both loved and cherished.

' on a hill far away, stood an old rugged cross the emblem of suffering and shame, and i love that old cross where the dearest and best for a world of lost sinners was slain.so ill cherish the old rugged cross till my trophies at last ill

Lay down.i will cling to the old rugged cross, and exchange it someday for a crown.Troy begins to gently sing this beautiful song.On a hill far away, stood an old rugged cross, the emblem of suffering and shame .then in a lou

der voice the officer driving the car joons in. and i love that old cross where the dearest and best for a world of loss sinners was   slain.So I'll cherish the old rugged cross till my trophies. At last I'll lay down, I will cling to the old rugged cross and exchange it someday for a crown. One of my favourites, the officer smiles and says. Really?asks Troy. Yes, I got saved 5 years ago . The church my wife and I attend sings a lot of old hymns and that's one of them. Well that's lovely replies Troy!!! Thanks, god will be with you today mr. Lewis,dont forget that. I wont Troy smiles and says.as the officer drops Troy off at the prisoners entrance

Troy is met by 3 individuals, an officer of the court ,a massachusetts state trooper and another young us marshall.Mr Lewis, your attorney is in the courtroom waiting for you,says the young trooper. Ok thank you, replied Troy. Also I'm gonna be sitting with you all day throughout proceedings. This is us marshall , marshall brian timson. Nice to meet you gentleman . you as well they both reply.marshall timson will be sitting directly behind us and there are 2 more plain clothes troopers in the court room.As all 4 men make there way down the hall Troy asks them why so many officers and marshalls? Troy says us marshall timson , this is court officer david landers massachusetts state trooper dylan jones and you already know my name. Mr Lewis,david dylan and i have all took oaths to uphold the law. And all 3 of us try and intend to do that everyday.mr Lewis if it's true that the fbi is in cahoots with the abiluabliqal drug cartel, you are on very very dangerous ground. What we intend tell serve honour and protect today.and to get to the truth!!! Thank you says Troy. I prayed and asked god no matter what happens to be with me today. Keep praying mr Lewis, keep praying says trooper dylan jones.

As they enter the courtroom Troy sees mr ralph lunsden mr lunsden good morning Troy says in his bright orange worcester mass prison coverallls. Good morning Troy i've got everything ready to go court starts in 15 minutes.

Troy is there anything else that you can recall from that night that may help us?

No sir, I've told you all that I'm able to recall. But i wonder if they jumped me for money or for another reason? What other reason could there be? Asks attorney lumsden. Well maybe the abiluabilqua cartel was trying to send a message to the Halifax boston cocaine syndicate. To knock me off as a message this is now all abiluabilqua cartel territory. Or maybe it was the fbi , knowing if they shut me up then there key witness against them would no longer exist, i don't honestly know.

Well i think it's best if we 100% go on a self defence proceeding.

Mr lunsden, i'd like to go with what you think is best sir.replied Troy.

I have prayed to god many times to help me. I believe he has sent you to me, to help me.well Troy i will do everything i can. As attorney lumsden looks at the clock on the wall he sees its 3 minutes to start time. As everyone sits in the courtroom and waits, Troy thinks to himself of the words written in the holy bible.Phillippians chapter 4 vs 13 to be precise. I can do all things through Christ which strengtheneth me.Lord grant me strength and wisdom for today is his final prayer , before court starts.

Chapter 9 ' the truth shall set you free!!

All rise.The honourable judge arnold smith preceding.You may be seated says judge smith to everyone in that courtroom today.ok docket no#Ma 275322 the state of Massachusetts vs Troy Andrew Lewis.Attorney flynn your opening statement please. Your honour we are here today to seek justice today for 2
Individuals that were attacked and one was murdered and the other one barely escaped with his life.Objection your honour replied attorney lunsden my client acted in self defense.Over ruled because we dont know of the events that actually took place but attorney flynn please dont be caught up in here say compared to facts. Yes your honour replied attorney flynn.Your honour we will

show through proof that this is exactly what has happened.the state of massachusetts is asking for the maximum sentence for these crimes we will prove in this courtroom today. Life without parole for the murder of samuel mateo garcia and 20 years without parole all served back to back for the assault with a weapon with intent to kill of fbi officer ricky alejaandro perez.
Attorney flynn.Yes your honour? I am well aware mr. parez and mr garcia were
Active duty fbi officers. I emphasise the word were. One gentleman unfortunately is dead and the other has been removed from active duty because of his injuries.ok your honour, thank you. Proceed young man.
We have evidence and witnesses to prove that Mr. Lewis   did not act in self defence but he purposely killed these men. That is all your honour thank you.

Attorney lunsden your opening statement please. Thank you your honour.
Your honour my client acted totally in self defense. Also if it may please the court, we will show evidence via the us marshals office that mr. Lewis is telling the truth.Objection your honour replied attorney flynn.There were no cameras in the rest area . Over ruled replies judge smith evidence comes in more ways than video recording.proceed attorney lunsden. Thank you your honour.We are seeking to prove today unequivocally that Mr . Lewis acted in total self defence. And we are requesting a full dismissal of all charges against him.Also your honour we have in   the courtroom today

2 key witnesses for the benefit of the court and Mr .
Lewis from the United States marshal's office.
Your honour, we thank you for allowing us to present
the facts and witnesses.
Attorney Flynn call your first witness please. Your
honour i call

 Ricky alejandro perez to the stand.as mr. Perez is
sworn in and takes a seat, the questioning begins.Mr .
perez how long have you been an fbi officer for
8 years before mr. Lewis attempted to kill me and i
wasn't able to perform my duties anymore.Objection
your honour.that is what is on trial today replied attorney
lunsdum. Agreed strike attempted to kill from the
record.Mr perez what is an fbi officers standard issued
weapon? A six shooter 38 hand gun.and on the nite that
the events took place you had this gun on you in
person? Yes sir. Yet you never drew it.That's right. Why
wouldn't a trained fbi officer in good standing not draw
his weapon in self defence. Because as i said me and
fbi officer Garcia was on our way home from work we
stopped to use the washroom. Mr Lewis was in a stall
and we were both facing the urinals relieving ourselfs .
He gently opended up the stall door, shot my partner,
then went for me.Your honour we call to the court's
attention evidence number 1. Mr Perez, you're a trained
FBI officer , what would you say this gun is? It looks like
a glock to me.that's correct. This is the same glock that
mr Lewis shot you with.
Your honour this gun was sent to an fbi lab and a us
marshals office lab for prints but they were wiped

clean.So we have no proof through prints for they were wiped clean.But mr. Lewis admitted and told the us marshals office where the gun was hid and buried in st stephen new brunswick Canada.who notified the rcmp who found the weapon and turned it into the us marshals office for evidence. Does this look like the glock used that night? Exactly like it. Thank you. No further questions your honour.

Attorney lunsden your witness.Mr perez for something that supposedly happened so quickly you wasnt long identifying that gun with certainty were you? Thats right thats because its the one he used .Objection your honour he's badgering my client.your honour i'm merely trying to establish mr perez is lying through his teeth. Your honour please mr garcia is dead and mr perez sustained horrible injuries.That stuff is par for the course in self defence!!! Your honour please,yells out attorney flynn.I will allow it. Mr. perez you are lying underoath to a massachusetts judge to me and certainly to mr Lewis.Ricky perez smiles at attorney lunsden ohh no no he chuckles and says. Your honour please he is baddering my witness. Your honour im not im simply trying to establish to this court through evidence may i add that this man is a bad man who did in fact try to kill my client.Over ruled. Proceed attorney lumsden.If someone tried to kill me and killed my partner in law enforcement
I certainly wouldn't be laughing and smiling as I'm on a court stand. Well it's just gonna be nice to see him get

what he deserves is all. Oh by god's grace and help someone will get exactly what they deserve mr . Perez, you.

Your honour may I present to you pictures of a young girl's emergency room visit? Yes. your honour what does pictures of some young girls emergency room visit got to do with this case?everything replies attorney lumsden.

Your honour please find enclosed 3 pictures of sonya anne leeds. As judge smith looks at them he says, what is the significance of these pictures she doesn't look hurt no but your honour she died 2 days after this because of drugs she had in her system.when miss leeds returned to the halfway house where she was living at the time all activities in that house is are video and Audio recorded at all times listen to what she says to the manager at 843 pm after returning to the halfway house the court officer instals the tape and presses play. Darell i don't feel so good. Well what did the emergency room ppl say? Thay pumped my stomach and figured they got the most of it out. There was a man stopped by here earlier replied the director to speak to you said you owed him 400 dollars. I don't owe anyone anything . He said he would be back tomorrow wanting his payment in full. Did he say his name? Yes, Ricky perez. Objection your honour shouts out attorney Flynn, what does this have to do with anything at hand here. Overruled replied judge smith.go on attorney lumnsden with your tape. Thank you your honour. He's with the abiuabilqua cartel replied sonya to the director can i see the tape of when he stopped by?

Sure says the director.your honour as you can see this is clearly mr. perez.

Your honour miss leeds died 2 days later . The autopsy report said it was from
Hardcore drugs in her system. Your honour, I'm trying to establish here that mr. Perez is certainly an active member of the abiluabilqua cartel.
Mr . Perez, the video doesn't lie, replied attorney lumsden what do you have to say about this?It was some lady on the street told me her name and where she lives needed $400 for food.i was just trying to help her out.
There are junkies everywhere i didn't know. You will know and understand fully
Once your sins catch up with you?

No more questions your honour.On and on witnesses are called but the last 2 witnesses attorney lumsden calls help to complete the case.its now well after 200 pm they took a half hour lunch break from 1130 am till 1200pm your honour i call Troy andrew Lewis to the stand.as Troy is sworn in attorney lunsden asks Troy all about the details of that night. I shut my car off and went to use the restroom. As I walked out of the restroom stall mr. garcia struck me in my face twice. As I hit the floor, Troy mr. Perez kicked my stomach .
I rolled over twice and quickly jumped to my feet.i pulled the glock from my pocket and fired upon mr. garcia.

As Mr Perez approached me he kicked my head and kept trying to reach in my pockets and take the money from me.he proceeded to get his hands around my throat . i feared for my life so i fired 2 shots on him.Any thing else you would like to tell the court mr Lewis?Yes replies Troy, i want it to be known these 2 men attempted to kill me. I was fighting for my life. Thank you.Attorny Flynn, your witness. Your honour the evidence is clear a known drug peddling thug mr. Lewis killed one man in cold blood and attempted to kill another.why? We don't know why , but perhaps it was in a drug induced rage.We have the weapon and we have the confession from mr. Lewis but I feel we have proven this to the court today.Your honour, we ask for fairness. Attorney lunsden do you have any other witnesses? Yes, your honour just one more. Your honour, I call United states marshall Carl tozer. As us marshall tozer is sworn in,mr lumsden asks him a very specific question.us marshall tozer,you have been leading an investigation that spans 4 states united states troopers office,s the us marshals office and the Halifax police dept of Halifax Nova Scotia Canada sir? Yes attorney lunsden that is correct.We have discovered that the abiluabilqua cartel has in fact infiltrated the fbi office of the united states.objection your honour what does this have to do with mr .Lewis,s trial.Overruled attorney lunsden may ask us marshall anything about an ongoing investigation when it comes to this case. Thank you your honour replies attorney lunsden.Marshall tozer what have u learned as per your investigation. We have learned that the FBI has been infiltrated by the abiluabilqua cartel. Mr. Garcia and mr. Perez were active gang members.

Marshall tozer are free to tell the court as to what has happened via the US marshal's office. Yes sir , the head director for the fbi east coast division has been brought up on racketeering , obstruction of justice , and intent to distribute and sell illegal drugs.Other arrest have been made in the case and

We are not done yet.marshall tozer is there anything you would like to tell the court concerning this trial? Yes there is. Your honour, the US Marshals office has been investigating corruption within the FBI for years now. The night samuel mateo garcia got shot and the night mr.ricky alejandro perez got injured, i have unequivocal proof and evidence that thay did go into that restroom in haverhill massachusetts that night to infact murder in cold blood Troy andrew Lewis.Objection your honour the us marshalls office couldnt possibly have evidence of this.Hold on one moment district attorney flynn.Attorney lumsden

You have this evidence with you in my courtroom today?

Yes sir your honour i present evidence from the us marshals office of a recording device hidden in the car of fbi agents and active abiluabilqua cartel members, samuel mateo garcia and ricky alejandro perez. Please press play marshall tozer replies judge smith.

 Why do they have us tailing this loser anyway ricky? When he stops he's toast as a message to the Halifax boston syndicate!! This is now abiluabilqua territory!!!!

Man what a great scam we got going Samuel some rat fink job with the fbi a perfect cover to sell drugs!!!! Ha ha ha for sure!!!! Hay , hay he's pulling over !!! lets rob him before we kill him? Ha ha ha ha good idea!!! More beer money for us!!!! We already got 24 on the backseat not anymore ricky i drank 5 of them!!! Hay your breaking the law!!! What are u gonna do arrest me fbi agent? Lets go rob this clown and then kill him!!! Ok!!!
Your honour the tape goes silent from then on it was a 6 hour tape and had been recording for 4.5 hrs which makes sense your honour. For they were found almost 1 hour later and their car was taped off by police 2 hrs later the tape had gone to the end.mr. Garcia and Mr . Perez never knew that there was a recording device planted within the car.

Your honour as you can see a blatant disrespect to the fbi and a blatant disregard for life. And obviously a blatant disrespect for Mr Lewis.
Attorney lunsden anything else? Judge smith asks. Yes one more thing your honour.If it would please the court mashall tozer has an arrest warrant for the arrest of ricky alejandro perez, for the attempted murder of mr Troy andrew Lewis. That is all your honour. Marshall tozer may i see the arrest warrant please? Certainly your honour. Judge Smith looks at it and hands it back to the U.S. marshall tozer.attorney flynn do you wish to cross examine. No no your honour.Bailiff please remand mr. perez into custody immediately and place him into the holding cell until this trial is over. Yes your honour replies the bailiff.Marshall tozer is any of your men in my

courtroom today? Yes your honour 3 men plus myself for a total of 4 of us.Bailiff take 2 of marshall tozers men and now remand Mr . perez into custody!! Yes your honour replies the bailiff. As the bailiff and 2 u.s. Marshalls take Ricky alejandro perez into custody, and places him into the holding cell until the court is adjourned judge smith makes an announcement.Attorney lunden , District attorney flynn , i'm gonna take a 10 minute recess. The court is in recess till then . Ok your honour replies both attorneys.after 5 minutes the 2 marshalls return to the courtroom.after 5 minutes judge arnold smith comes in and takes his chair.

The bailiff stands to his feet and makes his announcement.All rise, the honourable judge Arnold Smith presiding.You may be seated replies judge smith.Ladies and gentleman i am now ready for my sentencing of Mr . Lewis.
Attorney lunsden and Troy rise to their feet as sentencing is passed.
Troy andrew Lewis for the murder of samuel mateo garcia , i find you not guilty.
Troy andrew Lewis for the assault with a weapon and attempt to kill chagres
Against you to ricky alejandro perez i find you not guilty.
Troy starts to
Smile big and brightly. Attorney lunsden smiles and makes a fist with his right hand and motions it forward twice. Time served and all charges are dropped and

dismissed against you Mr. Lewis.Thank you, thank you your honour. Your welcome young man the judge smiles and says. Troy grabs a hold of his attorney and hugs him!!! Thank you sir. Your welcome, he smiles and says. And Mr. Lewis . Yes sir ,Troy replies. Dont forget god helped you today don't ever forget your commitment to him, it's called mercy and grace. I won't sir and thanks for the reminder.your welcome young man.

Us marshall Carl Tozer walks over to Troy. Mr Lewis i told you i would do everything i can to help you do u remember? Yes sir i did. Troy smiles and says.

Here is a bus pass to anderson south carolina and a voucher to days inn witch

Is 4 blocks from here.Thank you for everything marshall tozer. The bus station is 2 blocks the other way from Days inn. Make sure you're there at the bus station tomorrow morning at 930 am sharp. There's only 1 southbound bus per day and it leaves at 10 am sharp every morning.i will be Troy smiles and says.

Troy I want you to know the US marshal's office, Canadian rcmp , Halifax regional metro police and massachusetts state troopers are not gonna file or pursue any more charges against you. You are a free man. Thank you sir. Be in the lobby of your motel at 530 pm sharp to , your chicken dinner will be delivered to you.Thank you sir.God bless you Troy.Troy extends his hand and shakes marshall tozers hand.A s Troy walks out of the courtroom down the stairs and out of the court building, he takes a big breath of fresh air.

He thinks to himself , this is the best day for next days of the rest of my life. Troy walks over to days inn and checks into his room. H e picks up his phone and makes a collect call to olivers country store. Olivers country store lacey speaking, how may i help you? Yes operator ill accept a collect call from Troy Lewis. Lacey , Lacey sweetheart how are you? Hay sugar plum im fine how are you? Im great!!! We've been praying alot for you!!! I know god heard and answered your prayers!!!!! I've been totally cleared off all charges sweetheart!!!! Ahh sugar plum that's wonderful!!!! Yep the continental breakfast here starts at 7am . im gonna eat it then then immediately walk to the bus station dear for the southbound bus leaves at 10am sharp.

Well you call the minute you arrive and i'll come get you sugar plum!!!

Thanks!!! And thanks for praying for me!!!! Please say hi to Shirley and randy for me and thank everyone including them for praying for me!!!

I will sugar plum!!!!

Chapter 10; a new day is dawning.

As Troy looks out the window of his bus and sees the sign that says Anderson 33 miles, he gets a huge smile upon his face!! The dawn is breaking and the sun is coming up big and bright!!!! Troy says a silent prayer in his mind to God.

God thank you so much for getting me home safe , thank you for the great people you have brought into my life!!! People like randy and shirley and lacey!!!! God, I am glad to be free!!! Open the doors you would like me to go through, And shut the ones, That you don't want me to.I ask all this in the name of Jesus amen.As the bus pulled up to the bus stop, Troy didn't have to make any calls!!!!Lacey , randy and laceys grandma rhonda was all standing by the bus stop entrance door.As Troy gets off that old greyhound he immediately runs over to them all. And hugs each and everyone of them!!! When it was laceys turn she gives him a big ole peck on the cheek and smiles and says welcome home sugar plum!!!! Hay where is Shirley ? asks Troy.

Somebody had to mind the store while we were over here randy chuckles and says!! Let's go see her!!!

As they all go into Oliver's country store , Randy grabs 4 bottles of lemonade out of the coolers. Shirley is so happy and smiling and excited that a tear rolls out of her eye as she hurriedly runs around the counter and hugs Troy!!!!
Oh Troy dear welcome home, welcome home!!!!! Randy gives them all a bottle of lemonade, here you go everybody!!!! Troy smiles and says i am home im home and i'm free!!!!
In Jesus you sure are sugar plum!!!!!
As they drink their lemonade and talk, Shirley goes back behind the counter cause the store is getting busier and busier.
Lacey you enjoy your day today with Troy I will, lacey smiles and replies.
I got you scheduled to come in at 8 am tomorrow morning.
Ok Randy lacey smiles and says.Troy when are u ready to go back to work on the farm?asks shirley.
How about 4 am tomorrow for the milking? Ooh that sounds wonderful says
Shirley!! Ill say!!! Randy smiles and says. You know guys up in massachusetts
In january the day of my trial
 It was 23 degrees.ys well it is New England in the winter. Randy chuckles and says.No you dont understand, says Troy. This morning here its 908 am

and it's 64 degrees already. I know we are in the south, but in my heart you people make me feel warmer!!!!

Ahh, sugar plum that's sweet!! Well i thank god for all he's done for me and the
2nd chance he has given me!! For our light affliction which is but for a moment ,worketh for us a far more exceeding and eternal weight of glory.
2nd Corinthians 4 :17 Lacey smiles and says.
Hay that's right, replies Troy!!!! I read 1st and 2 nd Corinthians a lot while you were away sugar plum!!!
Wow he sure works in mysterious ways Troy smiles and says. Randy smiles and says he's a good god!!!Amen Troy replies.
Well Troy and lacey have a lovely day together and the next thing you know winter turns to spring spring to summer and then summer to fall!!

Randy hurry up honey the wedding starts in 1 hour the best man shouldn't be late now. I hear you dear. I'm just finishing up combing my hair.
You know I'm so proud of both those kids sweetheart!!!
God did great things for those kids Shirley . He sure has and he will continue to sweetheart!!
Randy and Shirley pull up to a packed church parking lot!!!!
As Randy walks in he sees Troy smiling randy, randy hi!!! Hi Troy you're looking mighty dapper there young man!!
Ha ha ha chuckles Troy smiles and says you look very nice!!!

There are 2 older people smiling at Troy and Randy standing about 10 feet away.

Randy, I would like to introduce you to my mom and dad Tommy and Helen Lewis. Very very nice to meet you, Randy smiles and says!!!! Helen looks at Randy and gently kisses him on his cheek and says to Randy, thank you for everything you have done for our son. Tommy shakes randy's hand yes randy thanks so much!!! It's my pleasure. Well it's just about time better take your seat mom and dad!!! We will son.

Well the wedding begins. Lacey walks down the aisle and looks radiant and beautiful!!! After Troy and lacey say i do and pastor tom pronounces them husband and wife, the next thing you know 8 years have flown by. Life and god have been good to lacey and Troy. 2 years and 1 month and 2 days after they said i do god gave them a beautiful little girl who they named ruth anne Lewis. 9 months ago they brought there 17 month adopted son home. His name is randy allen Lewis. Named after his godfather randy allen oliver.

These days lacey passes her time by singing in her home church and other churches in the south carolina area. Why just last month lacey got invited to a church in redding Pennsylvania to sing in a sunday morning and sunday evening service. Lacey still works for randy at the store a little less hours these cause she is a busy mama with little randy and ruth anne.

Troy still works on the farm for randy and shirley and for the last 4 years he has taught the 8 to 10 year old age range in sunday school on sunday mornings.Troy volunteers 1 saturday afternoon and evening a month at the local homeless shelter in anderson south carolina. He helps prepare and cook supper and then after supper and the dining hall dishes and clean up of the dinning hall .Everyone goes into the gymnasium and Troy gets behind the pulpit and preaches the word of god.By Troys efforts he has seen many people repent and ask Jesus into their heart and life!!! And he has seen many make a new fresh start too. God's word tells us in 1st thessalonians verses16 to 21 tells us. 16 Rejoice evermore. 17 Pray without ceasing. 18 In everything give

Thanks: for this is the will of God in Christ Jesus concerning you.

19 Quench not the spirit. 20 Despise not prophesyings. 21Prove all things;hold fast that which is good. Well Troy and all the souls that make a new start in the Lord Jesus Christ . Thank goodness for Jesus and his blood and grace and mercy and love!!! Mercy, grace and love. All things which each and everyone of us can find if we are on the road to redemption.

Frederick Demerchant

www.ingramcontent.com/pod-product-compliance
Lightning Source LLC
Chambersburg PA
CBHW051006140626
46546CB00016B/1012